GW00503534

THE LAWS OF MONEY

How to Use the Seven Spiritual Laws for
Wealth & Success

GULL KHAN

Copyright 2021 by Gull Khan.
All rights reserved. No portion of this book may be reproduced mechanically, electronically or by any other means, including photocopying, without written permission from the publisher. It is illegal to copy this book, post it to a website, or distribute it by any other means without permission from the publisher.

GYK Enterprises Ltd

20-22 Wenlock Road,

London, England,

N1 7GU

https://gullkhan.com/

Email gull@gullkhan.com

Limits of Liability & Disclaimer of Warranty

The author and publisher shall not be liable for your misuse of this material – this book is strictly for educational and information purposes only.

Warning and disclaimer

The purpose of this book is to educate and to entertain. The author and publisher do not guarantee that anyone following these suggestions, techniques, tips, ideas or strategies will achieve a particular result. The author/publisher shall have neither liability or responsibility to anyone with respect to any loss or damage caused, or alleged to be caused directly or indirectly by the information contained in this book.

Dedication

In loving memory of my mother, whose courage, principles, determination and strength of character have always been my inspiration. For my daughter, Maira and son Ayaan, who have both simultaneously motivated me and have been my strength in the toughest times in my recent years.

What other People Say About Gull

I can't begin to tell you how excited I am on this path! The great ways I can help others and volunteer with my time and money. I love that I can sleep good at night! Our trips allow us to enjoy family time and experiences. Now I can change my children's mindset and shifting their energy!

— Kristy Smith

Gull's teachings are amazing. I followed her steps and saw immediate results by day 2 of the mastermind challenge. Her energy is a ray of light and her stuff WORKS!!!

— Brigette Love

Had my session with Gull and I have to say she is an energy wizard! I found her tool for cutting ties with someone who was leeching my energy – excellent. I had a huge breakthrough in being able to break free without second guessing myself that it was time to cut loose from this person. But more than the tools and her expertise, I believe it's Gull's own energy that makes her so powerful, unique; inimitable and compelling. She is compassionate, non-judgmental, hilarious and kind. To me she exemplifies INNER AND OUTER WEALTH which is not easy to come by.

Gull got right down to the nitty gritty of what was hidden from my awareness with lightning speed and helped me to see clearly exactly what needed to shift. I am very careful who I allow to work on my energy and found Gull to be highly respectful and sensitive to this. I'm on the case with her recommendations and hugely grateful. Thank you lovely Gull.

— **Louise Smart**

She is a super powerful woman having lots of divine energy. I have been a part of one of the groups and that changed me - a lot of difference in my life. All her videos are amazing and its influenced not only me but also others. I highly recommend to watch her videos if you haven't been gone through yet. In my opinion she is one if the top energy and money healer in the world. Thanks Gull for adding me a part of your group.

— **Kris Nair**

I've just completed the Millionaire Mindset 5 day Challenge and felt truly uplifted throughout... today I had the abundance clearing call and found the experience really moving, despite believing myself to be an emotionally tough cookie, I was really moved by the experience and revelations through this call. Gull is really talented at being able to tap into the core issues. I'm looking forward to working with her to break through those issues. I feel like the process of change has already begun. Gull has opened up my mind to new possibilities where I thought there were none. If you're feeling stuck and needs some change I would really recommend some time with Gull.

— **Tigi Ghaffar**

This is a recommendation for coaching with Gull Khan.

2 years ago I invested 11 thousand pounds with a renowned marketeer/law of attraction personality who has worked alongside at least one big name from the movie "The Secret".

The coaching was for just over a year. Having only 2/3 skype calls in 2 months, he created a number of excuses not to call me as we originally agreed...this carried on for a few months, and then he completely went AWOL. What I learned from him was non originality from ideas he presented, and not worth the price he commanded.In comparison Gull Khan's 5 day free challenge was 100 times more effective. If this is 5 days, I can only wonder what the progress will be for clients at the end of their coaching experience... I will now whole heartedly suggest to others to take the limited opportunity of the personal one to one phone call with her, it's a great opportunity to finally decipher your money making journey...

Having already experienced the call myself, it is straight to the point, no jargon, no complications.

Why I recommend coaching:

> **Original Techniques.*
> **Practical.*
> **Easy access to reach her.*
> ** Fine tweaking your Goal.*
> **Creating powerful mindset.*
> **Emotional resonance to ongoing success.*

— Asgar Mozaic

Gull is amazing. I had a call with her and it was so easy to relate to her. I know she is coming from a place of love and really wanting to help people. She's amazing at what she does and can provide so much insight and clarity to what you need to do and change within your own life.

— **Jen Fontanilla**

Gull Khan is a powerful and deeply transformative mindset coach and energy worker, with techniques that I have never seen before! And I have experienced a lot of excellent energy work!

She is generously giving both her useful, excellent, and no BS knowledge, as well as her strong healing energy. She wastes nobody's time and speaks openly and directly of all essential matters around money problems people often have, even in her free challenges. I can really say that Gull Khan is a unique pearl and a shiny, powerful star in the sky of mindset coaches and energy workers! I hope to work with you more.

— **Anastasia Heidi M. Larvoll**

Gull Khan is brilliant. She is the Rolls Royce of Money Mindset experts. Enjoy the 5 days challenge and see for yourself how fast things start improving...

— **Melanie Detry**

Gull Khan is an amazing woman.

She shares so much knowledge, tools and techniques and she genuinely knows her stuff. She is honest and transparent. What you see is what you get with her. She has a beautiful spiritual gift and bless her for sharing it with the world. Her free five day challenge is amazing and a real eye opener. She really does shift your energy to a higher vibration. I highly recommend Gull if you are looking to becoming more spiritual and removing your money blocks.

I know I will definitely be working with Gull in the near future.

— **Debbie Singh**

Gull's coaching is brilliant. She has this innate ability to explain concepts simply and clearly. She is very knowledgeable and passionate. The tools she shares are simple and effective! Thank you very much!

— **Neelam Rai Kaul**

Contents

FOREWORD

In the past years that I have known Gull, not only have I benefited vastly from her immense intuitive knowledge in money related matters but I am personally very inspired by her brave and courageous journey - the journey of a single mom who started from ground zero but with dedication and excellence has built for herself an empire of loyal followers and clients.

As I have also quoted in my book Her Way to the Top, the first time I realised I may have limiting beliefs around money was a couple of years back, when I attended Gull's financial manifestation class. In that class, she asked us to write down our dream income. Many of us, including myself, hesitated to pen this down. In the next exercise, she asked us to double the income. And that's when almost all of us became terrified and uncomfortable. When she started exploring as to why we were uncomfortable, it turns out it wasn't because we thought the income was unattainable or overambitious, but we were scared to confront the changes that will come along with it. Most feared that they might not be able to justify time and commitment to their family once they started earning that much. Some were nervous about family reactions. Some even deliberated if their husband will be comfortable if they started earning twice as much. And then there were others who thought that their 'niceness', or perhaps the perception of it, might be impacted if they started earning a lot.

It was through Gull that I managed to identify energy blocks linked with my business income which I never knew I had! I also learned the importance of savings and healing from past traumas, a big one for me being my father's sudden death many years ago. Moreover, I was finally able to accept that not only was I fearful of failure but I was also nervous about success and higher earnings. This was a life changing discovery. I am also very lucky to have Gull as the core team member of International Women Empowerment Events. In the subsequent sessions that the IWEE team did with Gull, we learned the power of manifestations and guided visualisations and the clearings the team regularly did with Gull really enabled them and the organisation to attract abundance and achieve ground-breaking results. Gull, through innovative and transformative techniques, taught us how to distance ourselves from debilitating barriers that we had internalised over years and she positively changed our relationship with finances.

And I therefore say with conviction that this book content will most definitely have a positive impact on your life and attitude as it is had on mine and hundreds of others. If you are ready to transform negative energy and emotions, rewire your brain and change the way you think about money and unblock the flow of energy to get you to a higher frequency so that you start attracting all the goodness you deserve, then this book is just the toolkit you need.

— **Hira Ali**

Author of the Best-Selling Book "Her way to the Top"
Author | Writer | Speaker | Executive & Leadership Coach | Diversity & Inclusion Advocate | Chief Executive Officer of Advancing Your Potential

INTRODUCTION

My name is Gull Khan, and I am a Money Mindset expert. I've a happy, fulfilling life and a best friend who always helps me when I need her, namely Money. It wasn't always this way though, let me start by sharing my journey; how I went from being a banking and finance lawyer, to a money mindset expert, and everything that happened in-between.

This wasn't an easy journey. Nor was it a straightforward decision, or something I initially set out to do with intent. In my youth I had all the aspirations of becoming a world-renowned lawyer, but none for becoming a money mindset expert, none at all. The things I have learned, the journey that I've had and the experiences along the way are all what led me to where I am right now. I know I'm on the right path, and this is why I'm so passionate about what I teach. I'm passionate about money. I'm passionate about teaching the concept of money to the people around me; to my clients, friends and family. It is this passion which allows me to get the results for my clients that I do, and I have phenomenal testimonials to prove that my strategies actually work.

First though, I must recount the events that led me here, my lived life so that you understand what, and how, I understand. Foremost, I can assure you I understand the concept of not having money, and the feelings that go with that. However well off I might be now, it isn't where I came from. All will be revealed very shortly.

Let's start with the beginning. I was actually originally born in Manchester. My family moved to Pakistan when I was a few months old because my father wanted to set up a new business there. In Islam, Muslim men are allowed to have more than one wife. However, they expressly need permission from the first wife. My father did not ask this permission (my mother would have refused anyway) when he remarried. So, upon finding out he was with someone new, my mother left my father and we came back to the UK. My parents separating happened when I was five years old. My father played the financial card; by not supporting my mother, he assumed she would eventually come back, being used to a lavish lifestyle as she was, and that she would bring the kids back too. Unfortunately for him, my mother was a stubborn woman, and simply said, "Nope." Back in England, we found ourselves in London.

I grew up on a council estate in the East End of London. If you know anything about the East End of London, you can imagine what kind of life I had as a young child, being the kind of person I was. My brother was older than I, he went off the rails and did all sorts of unruly things; all because he couldn't adjust to the fact that we'd had lots of money, and now we didn't.

I went the other way. I wanted to prove to my father that I didn't need him, that I could be someone, and something, without his help or guidance. I studied hard. I was a straight A student, and I went on to pass university despite being assessed as severely dyslexic in the first year of my law degree. I was shocked by the fact that I was able to get such high grades despite my dyslexia. I still am - you can't change that. (There isn't a cure, not that I need one.)

When I look back, I realise now; all these achievements actually proved, was the fact that I was really hostile, all I cared about was getting to the level of my father - becoming a 'successful' and 'wealthy' person. I did it the only way I knew how back then; which was to study really hard and become a professional, such as a doctor, or a lawyer, or whatever else. I chose law because I'm very articulate, I speak well and have confidence, and therefore I chose a vocation that utilised those skills.

I went on to become not only a lawyer in the UK, but to qualify in other jurisdictions as well. I became a Barrister with a Middle Temple in the UK. I also became a New York Attorney. I actually passed the American bar exam prior to becoming a Barrister in the UK, but I didn't take the Hypocritical oath. I took the oath after, and therefore actually qualified as an Attorney after I became a Barrister with the England and Wales Bar Association. Because of the extensive experience I accumulated working for some of the top law firms in the world, let alone the UK, my experience was accepted by the Law Society and I became a fully qualified Solicitor with the England and Wales Law Society later on.

This means now I'm one of those rare breeds who is qualified as an Attorney, with the New York Bar, as a Barrister with Middle Temple, and also as a fully qualified Solicitor. That said, I practice in none of these disciplines today.

Once I became a lawyer, my career was my mission. I lost my mother when I was 21 years old, and that loss led me on the path of being even more determined to be successful and focussed, to stand ahead of everyone else. I was determined to attain a lot of success, despite things that might hold me back such as personal loss, or my dyslexia. It was this thinking that led me on the path of personal development; I first went ahead and picked up a Tony Buzan book about mind maps that I read after finishing a speed reading course, all of which helped me study and excel further. I also picked up another Tony authored book; this time Tony Robbins' *Awaken the Giant Within*. It was this that led me on my long journey of becoming a personal development junkie; I'd already been a personal drama junkie and had been doing that for quite some years.

Now, I had no intention of ever going into personal development. It was just something I studied to allow myself to have personal success, and succeed societally, in the way I wanted to. Like I've said; I was very determined to have financial success. By the time I was in my mid-20s, I was working for some of the top law firms in the world, earning high figure salaries in both pounds and dollars, all with the respect of my peers.

Once all this was achieved, I chose to have an arranged marriage. Yes, I went down the traditional path of actually having an arranged marriage. My father chose my first husband for me. We only had meetings a couple of times before the ceremony. My first husband decided he didn't want to work, he preferred to be able to be a stay at home husband who would look after our new-born daughter. I was happy about this. He did a little bit here and there, but most of the financial burden was on me, which was fine, I was happy to accept because I was a banking finance lawyer on a good salary.

I worked exceptionally hard and was able to become a property entrepreneur on the side. I manifested a million pound property portfoliowhilstworkingfulltime,andbeingpregnantwithourbabygirl. However, the more financially dependent my husband became on me, the more physically abusive and controlling he became towards me, until I found myself in a dangerous and abusive marriage. I stuck with him at first, for our daughter's sake, but he eventually became so abusive and violent it didn't matter if our child was present or not and after I finally plucked up the courage to call 999 that was the end of the marriage.

During the separation from my first husband I fought for everything through the courts, and I was able to safeguard all my property because we had been married for less than two years. This, along with my proving the fact that it was an abusive marriage meant the courts were on my side and I retained my independent wealth. Nonetheless, I remarried. I thought I had now learned my lesson - not to allow a man to become financially dependent on me. I at least thought that this time around; in a second marriage, I would be better off. My second husband had been 'interested' in me, in love with me so to speak, for the previous sixteen years prior that we'd known each other so I accepted the semi arranged marriage proposal. It wasn't that we dated or I got to know him for a very long time, I just went from one marriage to the next. In this second marriage my husband did take 'care' of me. He decided he wanted me to be a stay at home mom, rather than continue going to work, and I was happy to accept. He seemed willing to put the effort in, things felt stable, and despite giving up my law career I was fulfilling my personal development and manifesting money through him. He set up his business and very quickly went on to earn five figure monthly profits. I retained my property portfolio that I had earned prior to this marriage.

During this second marriage, my husband was adamant he wanted me to stay home. So I did, I stayed home with my daughter and a couple of years later with a son we had together as well. This marriage was never physically abusive, but over time he became verbally aggressive and began belittling, as well as making me financially dependent by design. He was adamant I could not work and the more I stayed at home, the less I could do, until I began to lose my confidence. He threw constant verbal abuse, killing everything about me until he'd completely destroyed my internal character. I went from being someone who was confident in their mental and intellectual capability, who was confident of the fact that she could achieve unlimited financial success to becoming a housewife in a second abusive marriage. The question here would be how could I have allowed that to happen? Why would I choose to be a stay at home mom who didn't work?

Let's look back, because I want you to remember that by the age of twenty-one, I had lost my mother. A woman who raised me, who was my whole world. I was desperate to have my own family, to fill the void her loss left.

My second husband decided he wanted us to just focus on my daughter for the time being, while constructing an ideation of what our future family would be like. And then later on, when we had a son together, he didn't want me to 'waste my time' outside, or doing something from home, he wanted me to wholly focus on our family while he supported us. As ambitious as I am, previously family was not my priority and so I fell in line with this thinking, because at the end of the day, we all want love and I really lost the love of my mom. And I wanted to make sure that my children had their mother's love as much as possible. So, this is where the motivation came from, and the decision to stay at home.

So, I accepted but of course there's always a twist, isn't there? The more financially dependent I became on him, the more verbally abusive he became towards me - I'm fat, I'm ugly, I'm stupid, and the like. He personally wasn't very educated, and he felt serious resentment about me being well educated and my intellectual status, the fact that I was allegedly 'arrogant'. I was consistently belittled and made to feel as small as possible so he could excerpt control as much as possible.

I found out later on that he was a textbook narcissist. Everything I have described is the typical behaviour of a narcissistic man. However, I didn't know this at the time so I believed there was something wrong with me. Despite his controlling behaviour and the constant put downs I did try to continue with personal ventures, I desperately tried doing things like affiliate marketing, encouraged by false promises of how someone could achieve everything very easily, or at least could achieve a really good result. I went to someone who couldn't achieve anything but talk, however. Whatever I touched, whatever business opportunity I tried; it seemed like everything turned to dust. No business opportunities worked for me at all. My husband even invested, finally, some money with me which failed miserably, all our savings, everything went towards failure instead of success. Nothing I touched worked, none of our businesses, no ideas, nothing at all. I couldn't make a penny, and my husband held my life in his grip.

Simultaneously while this was going on, I was on another journey. I was trying to figure out my spirituality for the first time. I was at home around my kids but wanted more than to sit around watching

TV. So, I started the journey of understanding myself. I tried an alternative healing emotional therapy, known as the Emotional Freedom Technique. I learned, and trained up, until I became an expert in this field. I also learned about Reiki and then my final step was with intuitive healing. I studied with a renowned mentor; I was on a twelve-month program with her. When I did that, that's when I realised that I had this gift of energy healing and energy clearings. And it's these skills that I learnt during that time, which I use at the moment. The moment 'then' was not the positive moment I am in now, however, and though I was practicing and learning all of this throughout that time, so I was able to help people with my energy healings and performing energy clearings, I wasn't yet able to help myself. I was in a highly abusive marriage that completely killed off all my confidence in my personal ability, with my narcissist husband's intention being to do this as much as he could. It was my investigations into energy healing that literally helped me rise like a Phoenix from the ashes of my abusive second marriage and why right now, I'm a completely different person to who I was then. Nonetheless, at the time I had all these inner feelings that I couldn't be out of the marriage, that there's something wrong with me, as most females do when they're in an abusive marriage. But there was a light at the end of the tunnel and the light was given to me back in 2016 when I found out he was having an affair. We went on holiday to Disneyland, as a family, together for my daughter's ninth birthday. During that vacation I found out that he was 'seeing' a nineteen-year-old. So, I confronted him and we had this, obviously, massive argument. When we came back home we decided to separate, but not to divorce. We separated so we could work on the marriage. At that time, I felt there were cracks in the marriage not just because of him, but also because of me; that we somehow lost touch with each other and could try harder with the marriage and make it work. A few months down the line I realised that wasn't the case. He wasn't willing to come back home, and I couldn't walk away. Therefore, one night I had a conversation with Divine Source Energy (as in the very essence of however you feel God's energy, or the 'Divine Source' itself) that meant a door opened. It was on the thirtieth of August 2016. I remember going to sleep. I'd just taken my kids to a popular theme park here in London, and on the way back I was really happy and content with my kids, with how my life was, but I prayed to Divine Source Energy that night and said, "Just tell me what I'm supposed to do, tell me what it is with this individual? Could we work out things together? Are we meant to be together, or not meant to be together? Just give me an idea. Give me an indication of what's going on. What's wrong, I'm stuck. I need your help and guidance." I specifically remember making this prayer, I just left the question completely up to Divine Source Energy, "So; just give me a clear, short sign. What it is I'm supposed to do?" I didn't even expect an answer, at least not as clear as the one I received.

I awoke in the morning the following day, Monday the thirty-first of August and actually woke up late when normally I'm an early riser. I usually get up about six but that day I awoke at nine o'clock and the first thing I heard in my head was to go to where my husband was living. I knew the address, but I had never been there before. I had a very clear notion – go to where he's living. I remember arguing with myself not to, yet I had this very clear noise in my head, a voice saying - Go, you need to get out of the house, you need to be there before ten thirty. I couldn't say why at the time, but it stated this very clearly. I remember jumping out of the bed, putting on yesterday's clothes,

I didn't brush my teeth, or wash my face, just grabbing my kids and giving them milkshakes for breakfast which they drank in the car. We just shot out in the car and rode out of London; he was actually living in Luton at the time; about an hour and a half from where I was.

On the way there was no traffic, so we actually got there early; around a quarter past ten. Lo and behold; I'm knocking on the door and it doesn't open, even though his car's parked outside. I put a brick through the window to attract his attention and once the door was open found him in a compromised position - she was literally putting her clothes back on. I caught him red handed with this nineteen-year-old, this girl again, and that was the end of the marriage for me. He felt differently, openly wanted to keep both me and her, exactly the same deal as my father had wanted with my mother. This is a very important point I'm going to come back to later, so I need you to remember this. I left, and being a lawyer myself I did the prep work for the divorce and gave him the ultimatum that if he resisted I would file on the fact he cheated on me, but if he agreed to it, and we just ended the marriage based on mutual consent, that would be the end of it, and that's what we did. It was the end of marriage but he did the same thing that my father did – again a point to remember because I want to come back to this - he behaved the same as my father and played the financial card; refusing to give me any kind of child maintenance support or home support, refusing to pay the mortgages, he essentially refused to do anything. My kids were in private school at the time and I had to pull them out but he didn't care. Again, I must stress this is an important point to remember, one I'll return to in due time. But for now, I was alone apart from my children and, once again, I had to start from scratch.

Now, I'm sure you remember I became a property millionaire before I was thirty but this was shared with the husband I was divorcing, so please remember that as well. Being a property owner means I'm not eligible for financial support in the UK. Getting a divorce meant I couldn't touch the property because obviously it was equally divided between me and him, so I was pretty much stuck - being a property millionaire certainly, but in the meantime having literally no money to feed my children.

This was my lowest point. I remember sitting at my dining table and thinking - I've no money to my name. The only money that was coming to me was child benefit, due to living in the UK. This is less than one-hundred and fifty pounds every four weeks, and everything I had to look after my two children. That's the only money that I had, and I was sitting there thinking, "God, how am I going to feed my kids? How am I going to do anything? I have no clue."

At that moment I hadn't put the pieces together. I was still looking at individual elements and hadn't seen the bigger puzzle, I was yet to realise what it was that had happened, what action I needed to take. A relative phoned me, right at that very moment, and it was talking with my aunt, listening to Divine Source Energy talking through my aunt, that actually brought the real issue to my attention. She looked at my life. She looked at me; she listened to me telling her what had happened, what my husband had done and everything else. And then she came up and she said this to me, and it was this statement that changed my life. After listening to the entire story of what happened over the last few years, she turned around and said to me, "I'm so sorry this has happened to you, your mother must have turned in her grave. The same thing has happened to you as happened to her."

I remember how I thought - Huh, what do you mean? Come again? This was literally how I reacted to her, with confusion and disbelief. She spoke wisely of course, saying – "Gull; the exact same thing happened to your mother; the exact same thing is happening to you, it's such a shame that history is repeating itself".

I was floored, I had not until that point realised this honest truth and couldn't connect the dots to realise what had happened, what I'd let happen, to myself and my surrounding life. This is why I wanted you to remember what I said I'll come back to. I manifested my mother's entire life all over again, with myself as the shell to hold that manifestation. History absolutely repeated itself, all without me realising. The points were so obvious; it was absolutely amazing when I put them together. My father remarried around the time my mother was in her mid to late thirties, I was then in my mid to late thirties.

My father married a woman much younger than my mother. The girl my husband cheated on me with (and was going to get married to, I discovered later that if I hadn't caught them that day they were scheduled to get married at eleven o'clock, intending to leave at half past ten – the very time I knew I had to arrive for at the latest!) was the same sixteen years age difference with myself as my father's new bride was with my mother. When my father remarried, my mother had two children - a boy and a girl, of whom I was the younger one - and I was five years old. I had a boy and a girl, and my son was five years old. My father played the financial card as a means of manipulation; he'd wanted to keep both my mother and his second wife. My husband played the same monetary hand; he wanted to keep me and his girlfriend as well. Can you believe it? Can you imagine I manifested into existence my mother's exact life, to an absolute tee? It was really amazing to me, albeit a great shock in that moment of realisation.

Now, somebody else could sit and cry about it and think - Oh my goodness, what have I done? Personally; I actually felt liberated. Though the experience was hard while it was happening it was now over, and I found myself thinking - I've had to do this and that if you think about it; I had to make being a Barrister working in the UK happen, I had to make becoming a property millionaire happen and now I'm this lawyer whose become a victim, a single mother of two children being put through hell and everything else and I had to manifest all that too! Can you imagine the power that's required to manifest these things? Even if it is going from one extreme to the other, if I could do that - manifest my mother's exact life - what else could I possibly manifest? If I were to hone, and use, these manifestation powers correctly? You see my point. This was the most liberating moment of my life, up to that time. It was the turning point, where everything changed in my life. Divine Source Energy altered my perspective. It changed everything in that moment when I realised – if I can create this, I can create the life of my dreams. If I can create this, I can create anything! That is what I've gone on to do, and this is what I can help you to do too, in time.

Soon after that, I realised I had been on this journey for a long time. I was aware of limiting beliefs, I was aware of the law of attraction, I was aware of how things transpire, yet I was not applying it in my own life. And this is what had to change.

From that moment I made it my mission to unravel <u>every limiting belief,</u> every ideology about men, about money, about life, about success, and about myself that I could have. And within the space of literally six months, I transformed my life for the better in every way.

The first thing to happen was forgiving my ex-husband. We are friends now, because we are co-parenting our children, and for that reason I wanted to become friends with him. I don't want to have any ill feelings holding me back. So, we have a friendly, cordial relationship. Not just for the sake of the children, but because I know forgiveness is the path to prosperity. I really believe in that, so I forgave him. I worked on every aspect of myself. The first person I had to forgive was my husband, but the second person was myself; for creating all this mess, so I forgave him, I forgave myself, I forgave my father, I forgave everyone around me. I worked on all of my beliefs. I unravelled things, I came up with strategies. One of these, that was born in this time period, was my Three Steps to Cash Flow Mastery. You can listen to the Podcast at https://moneymindsetwithgullkhan.podbean.com/e/episode-10-mastering-cash-flow-for-abundance/ But for now, remember that's my famous strategy - Three Steps to Cash Flow Mastery. Everything I have told you so far is the reason why I'm so passionate about it. I know it works through my experiences, be they good or bad. It works for me, it worked for me back then, it works for my clients right now. It is so powerful that you have to adopt it, believe in it from your own self, as those who do reap all the rewards. I'll explain how it all works, this book will show you the path; the Three Steps to Cash Flow Mastery. First though, I'll finish my own story.

Now, because I had realised all this truth, I began to apply it to my own life; that being the life that was still a mess back then. I was running out of my savings very, very quickly. All the gold was sold; everything was sold in fact with nothing left behind. My kids were pulled out of the school. I was a single mother with no employment; I still had to find a way to make money. I realised at the time I had two options. I'd begun to unravel my life, work, and limiting beliefs, but I also had many other things to do. So, I had to choose my path. My initial option, also the most obvious, was to go back into practicing law, but there were some issues. The cons against me going back to this type of work included that I always hated law in the first place. I wasn't a big fan of the corporate world. Secondly, the prospect of working eighty to ninety hours a week while seeing my children infrequently made me want to vomit. My children already saw their father infrequently; I didn't want them to miss out on having their mother as well. But most of all, back then I was in the infancy of realising that if I can create a mess such as the one I was in personally, if I could manifest my mother's exact life, what else could I create? So, I became determined to create a successful business. Now keep in mind that up till now I'd never had a successful, personally run business. I'd had multiple failures, not just the affiliate marketing, but things such as setting up a physical care home that ultimately lost a hundred thousand pounds in capital, and various other businesses that had not made a single penny whatsoever. This was where my concept of toxic money was born. I realised this toxicity was why I had not made money in any of my previous ventures. I decided to work through my toxic money problem, and come out the other end, by setting up a successful, rewarding business, to which the question was; what would I do? What kind of business would I have? The most obvious idea was that I could do coaching, that as an intuitive healer I could therefore heal other people, not just myself. The question quickly became; what would I heal? Being a healer, specifically an energy healer, I can help physical relationships. I can do physical bodies, or whatever else. But the one thing that came to my mind, more than anything else, was I would heal people's money stories. That became the 'it' I sought, because I truly believe if you can solve your money story, you can solve anything. You know why? Because in order for you to solve your money story, you have to solve your emotional baggage, you have to go deep and face your deepest darkest demons, and unless you do that your money story will never get fixed and, at the very best, you will be stuck in a cycle of boom and bust where you may not be able to manifest anything or you may not be able to manifest much. There's always going to be those internal issues until you face your deepest, darkest demons; you cannot get to any desired level of wealth, achievement or success, and also do it with ease and grace, without first standing up to these demons.

At times I find people achieving success, but though they do it through hard work and diligence they're always hustling, always doing urgent things until they find themselves burning up or burning out completely. That is not what I wanted for myself, that's not what I wanted for my children and it's not what I want for you.

I realised I wanted to teach people to achieve money with ease and grace, to allow money to come to them, by creating a system, a program where the money starts coming to you, rather than you running after the money. This is when I came up with the concept of the money avatar. Because my first concept was: what if money was my best friend? How would she behave with me? How would I treat her? This is where the money avatar was born, because I wanted to help people become best friends with money. I will talk about your money avatar in a coming chapter. For now; this is where all these concepts were born. And this is how I went on to becoming a money mindset coach.I initially took on the title of expert, because when I started teaching people, and the kind of results people were getting, I actually realised that most people out there who are teaching concepts like the law of attraction are not really money mindset experts. They're simply not. I realised my tools, the strategies I employ were different. They worked for a reason; because I had lived through lack and scarcity, before coming out the other end, and had actually applied all these strategies to myself. I had to succeed because my biggest motivation was how to feed my kids? My motivation was not to get the next diamond ring, or to buy a new Ferrari. My motivation was how am I going to get food on the table for my family? My two young children. This is why I started, how I built myself up from rock bottom, and it's so powerful for you to understand, because you have to develop yourself as I developed myself.

Now, on this journey, I've gone from becoming a confident young individual, assured in her appearance and her mental capability as a successful lawyer, to becoming a stay at home mom completely devoid of any confidence whatsoever, be it in her physical appearance, her mentality, or her ability to create a functional, working business to finally becoming a money mindset expert, one who is again confident in her appearance, in her ability to help people and provide a service who knows that she can make a change in the world. This is who I've become now, and this story I have told is why I have become this passionate person.

I've had all this success because when I focussed all my energies on working out my money stories, everything around me changed – not just the way I am personally transformed, but also my relationship with Divine Source Energy is changed for the better because honestly, you cannot have a great relationship with money if you don't have a great relationship with Divine Source Energy. That's one of my core principles that I teach: in order for you to have a great relationship with money, it doesn't matter what name you give to Divine Source Energy, you can call it Buddha, Rama, you can call it The Universe, whatever name you give to Divine Source Energy is not my business, my business is that unless you have a great relationship with Divine Source Energy, you will never even have a good relationship, let alone a great relationship, with money. It's as simple as that.

You can hear in my writing how passionate I am about this. I want you to understand that money can be your best friend; not something that you reach out for or need to run after, not something that you crave if you come from that place of needy energy. I want you to have this passion for life, and for you to know that money is your best friend, the one who will always be there before you need it. A best friend that will always be there to support you and have fun with you as well. Money doesn't even have to live with you; please always remember there's the ebb and flow of money, money will come and go. But she's always there whenever you need your best friend, any time where it really counts. That's the kind of concept I want to bring into your life. That's the concept I want you to understand, that I'm going to teach you.

So, this is the purpose of this book. It is about me sharing my experiences, my teachings, all my considerable learnings about money. I became a money mindset expert, as you can see now, through my experienced ups and downs. There have been many ups, many downs and I've had many issues. Am I angry at anybody? Hell no! Am I upset with my ex? Am I upset with my father? No. Do I face my issues with confidence? Hell yeah!   I'm very happy where I am now and I wouldn't go back and change even one day of my life. Everything has led me to where I am right now, and I love where I am right now. I'm able to have the life of my dreams, I'm able to have an amazing relationship with myself, my kids and my clients. I serve my clients with authenticity, humility, and passion. I'm able to get them all the results they deserve, the things they want and I'm able to change people's lives. This is my mission in life and the story I've told is why I'm so passionate about it. I will soon be focusing on taking my abilities, on a pro bono level, to developing countries where I can help people with changing their mindset around money and improving every quality of their lives. For the time being though, as in right now, I'm focusing on helping YOU. Helping you through this book, with my podcast, my training, and especially through my expert, high end paid programs as well.

I hope you've enjoyed hearing my personal story and realise why I am where I am today. I started off as an independent, strong minded, professional lawyer and despite the setback's life offered, now I have ended up being this independent, strong minded, passionate money mindset expert. My sole focus of doing this book is to make sure that everyone who reads it builds a really strong friendship with money. I'm here to help you, and eventually you'll move on from me to be with the best friend you, or anyone, could ever have: money.

Chapter 1

IMAGINATION AND THE LAWS OF PROSPERITY

S o, you know who Gull Khan is and now we're here together to examine The Seven Laws of Money in this book. We're here with chapter one. I'm super excited about writing this exhilarating book. It's going to be packed with amazing value and content, so much so it's going to be fabulous. We are going to explore quite a lot of in-depth knowledge - so yeah, I'm glad you have been waiting because this will be worth the wait, I promise you. We start by covering foundational basics in this chapter, which I think is really important, so I'm going to go over what my understanding is, how I explain to my clients what I mean, who you are, what you are, your conscious mind and so forth.

Once we've done the foundation work first of all, over the coming chapters we will be covering one particular law in each chapter with regards to prosperity and how that fits in with you. It's like putting all the pieces together. I suggest you read through the entire book first, then come back for the second reading and take down notes because that's how I learn and remember. But first and foremost, you have the book you need in front of you if nothing else.

Okay; let me lay down the foundation work for you. We are going to cover the seven Universal Laws over the next seven chapters, hence the name The Seven Laws of Money. First, we're going to cover the foundational work over the next two chapters, which is essential. Don't skip these chapters; the content in these is absolutely worth its weight in gold. Without the understanding of this foundational work, you cannot actually apply the principles or utilise the Universal Laws of money. Therefore, this is essential for you.

I'm going to be talking about the power of imagination, why that's so powerful, and I'm going to be talking about the three minds you have and how to individualise them, what their respective roles are and how they each impact your life. I hope that's clear to you. We've got a jam-packed menu for you. This is the foundational chapter, but it's essential. You absolutely have to know all this before you can actually apply the principles of law.

Life - A Gift from God!

"Life is a gift from God, an unlimited series of opportunities to find the good in ourselves and others. There is good in everything, if we are willing to see it."
Alan Cohen

Alright, let's get straight into it. The first thing I want to get across to you is that this life of yours is a gift. I'm Muslim, so I can say that in my religion, people often refer to life as a test. They say that you're here to suffer through this existence and that God will give you a reward after all the tests you go through. Similar principles apply across Christianity and Judaism, as well as other religions. For now, I want you to understand that life is not a test. Life is a gift. That's the first thing you have to understand. It has rules – life is like a game. If you play by those rules, you win the game. If you don't play by those rules, you lose.

Consider gravity and aerodynamics: if you know how to manipulate these laws correctly you can fly like a bird, you defy gravity with a balloon before drifting slowly home by parachute, you can do everything. You can put those propellers on, soar high with rocket boots and jetpacks, you can fly. But you have to understand the rules of aerodynamics and gravity first. It's the same with Universal Laws of prosperity. There is no capricious God out there who's watching you do something bad and trying to make your life miserable. God is divine. God is loving. God is within you. I want you to understand that point first. This is coming from somebody who's utterly devoted to God. I don't wear the hijab, but that's the only thing I don't do. I fast, I adhere to all my religious rules: no alcohol, no haram food. Everything in my life is in line with Islamic principles. I can say this being completely devoted to God, but I don't use that in my teachings because I believe that everyone chooses their own path. My personal path is devotion to my God. This is why I can say that I don't believe there's any capricious God out there who's trying to cause you harm by making sure that you have a miserable life. Your life is a gift. That's the first thing you have to understand. But it comes with a set of rules. Everything has rules. There are rules for gravity, for prosperity, for your health and so forth. You have to understand these rules.

If this is not something you're familiar with, something you weren't aware of, I'm here to give you those rules right now. I'm here to help you. So the foundational work, before you can learn and accept the rules, you need to embrace the fact that life is a gift. There are certain rules - it's like playing a game, and you have to play by the rules or else you cannot win in the game. I'm not trying to offend anyone whose religious ideals differ - these are my personal views, so please take them with a pinch of salt. I have read the Old Testament, I have read the New Testament and I have read the Bhagavad Gita. So something else I want to clarify is when I take things from all different religious contexts, I can say it with authority, because I have read the Bhagavad Gita, I've read the Old Testament, I've read the New Testament and of course I've read the Quran, so I'm familiar with the religious context. That's why I love all religions as well, because all religions have the same purpose and destination. All religions lead to Divine Source Energy, even the modern-day secular ideology of the Law of Attraction and the Universe, which is another different path, it all leads to the same destination. Everything leads to a Divine Source of Energy. That's my take on it. There's a phrase in the Old Testament that I absolutely love: 'What every man soweth, that shall he also reap'. We've heard this time and time again. When the Old Testament says this, it is talking about deeds, but I take it in a broader context. I actually believe that intention is absolutely vital. Whatever you send out into the outside world, you will get back - not just your deeds, but also your intention.

So what is intention? Intention means your thoughts, your ideas, who you are, and what you intend. Therefore, thinking it's just the deeds you do and the actions you take is a very narrow perspective of what you're sending out into the world. Think of yourself as a satellite: you are sending and receiving information. In that context, whatever thoughts and ideas you're sending out, that is what is going to come back to you as well, because you're on that frequency. So when we are talking about the information you send out, it's in the broader context, not the narrow one - its thoughts, ideas, all along with your actions. You will have a lot more thoughts and ideas overall in your life, whereas actions are a narrower avenue of experience. You may have more than a thousand thoughts in an hour, but you may only take one or two actions. So you need to open your mind about what you're sending out to the world. It's broader. It's more than just your actions. It's your thoughts, ideas, your intentions as well. This means that if somebody lies, they get lies back. If somebody cheats, they get cheated on. If someone criticises other people, they get criticism back. This is where this rule becomes really, really powerful.

Imagination, Your Very own Power Tool!

"Imagination is everything, it's a preview of life's coming attractions"
Albert Einstein

Secondly, let's talk about your imagination. I believe imagination is our secret weapon and those people who understand this are really blessed, because your imagination is literally the greatest superpower that you have as a human being. Scientifically, what's the difference between me and a monkey, or a dog and a cat and a bat? Not much. There isn't much difference organically - we're all made up of organic matter. Our DNA is actually very similar to that of chimpanzees. So what is it that we have which differentiates us from our animal counterparts? The answer is imagination. Einstein put his imagination as the initial step that led him to investigate all his amazing scientific discoveries, he put all that down to his imagination as a way which allowed him to develop personally and bring so much goodness into the world. So if imagination is that powerful, and Einstein understood it and all these other great minds understand imagination, please remember that you and I have the same faculty; we all have imagination as a superpower... we all do. Now, if we don't use it, that's a different matter. But we all have it.

It's said that whatever you ideate with your imagination internally, sooner or later that same thing shows up externally. For example, we all know somebody who's always fretting about something like, 'there's always something wrong, there's always something wrong'. Well guess what, they'll produce something wrong. I'll give an example from one of my friends; she's always complaining that she gets food poisoning. She gets food poisoning all the time. We will all be sitting in the same restaurant; we'll all have the same food, but guess who will get the food poisoning? Seriously. Imagine there are four of us. Three of us wouldn't get sick. The only person who would get sick with food poisoning would be that one friend of ours. And she would say, "Oh, you know that restaurant's awful because of the food   poisoning it caused me." This is so important. Why? Because she's thinking about food poisoning. She's thinking of ways to get food poisoning. What if she focused on NOT getting food poisoning? This leads us to the realisation that we must train our imaginative faculties. Once they're trained, we can have every good thing we can possibly think of. However, understanding the power imagination holds is the second essential fundamental point to remember.

I'm going to delve into how the subconscious and all our different minds play into it, and how this becomes really, really relevant to you later. But let's stay focused on your imagination for the time being. If we can imagine everything, and everything we see we can imagine with our internal eyes, whatever we internalise we can therefore externalise. I've said this many times, whatever we hold internally, we manifest externally. These images are very important. Now, when people learn about the law of attraction, they say "yeah, I know this, I know this." Even if you've heard about the Law of Attraction before, you need to hear this AGAIN. If I'm here, if you're here, listening (or reading in this case) to me in this moment, that means you've attracted me into your world. There's an old proverb; when the student's ready, the teacher appears. Thus, if you're here, right now READING this, pay very close attention because I've been brought into your world for a reason. Do you need to hear this again? Why? Well let me ask you: how do we learn? Through repetition, repetition, repetition. This is why.

Therefore, listen to me very, very carefully. You need to hear this. Whatever is coming into your life right now is what you're imaging, consciously or subconsciously, it's as simple as that. Okay? You are actually manifesting every aspect of your life, the bill you just had, the parking ticket, the argument with the neighbour, the argument with your spouse, the argument with your child, your health, ailments, everything that you are actually manifesting in your external world is because of you; you are solely responsible. I do believe you have to take personal responsibility for <u>absolutely everything</u> in your life. That's such an important point. If you're not willing to take personal responsibility for everything that's showing up in your life, you will not be able to change it because then you will rely on external factors, some external law, some external Divine Being, some external something or other to actually change your life. The first thing you have to understand is that you are using your imagination to manifest everything externally - this is foundational principle, absolutely foundational. You have to actually accept it one hundred percent, no arguments, okay?

Everything outside - the death of a loved one, the birth of another and everything in-between, the accident, the house burning down, the dog running away, the cat coming in, all the good things as well, meeting your ideal mate, having that lovely dinner, tea with your daughter, your son or someone special - that is you creating it. You image that into your life. You use your imaging faculty to use your imagination. And you externalise it. And that's how it appeared.

Okay, that's super, super important for you to internalise and process. Understand this; because once you take personal responsibility for absolutely everything showing up, you can change your life. I'm going to give you an example I hope you remember from earlier, this hit me head on in my life, it really was the biggest life changing moment I've ever felt. I've shared the story before, I had manifested my mother's exact life and I wasn't even aware it had happened. In my thirties, a single mum with two children living in a very poor part of London, even though my background was as a lawyer qualified in three jurisdictions. I'm not going to go into my background again. And when that was happening, I didn't see it till it was done.

During that time, even though I knew about the law of attraction and I'd been studying prosperity. I was teaching it and working with clients pro bono as a hobby, sharing things with people. I was doing energy clearings. I was working with people. I was aware of this concept, I internalised it. However, I had not seen the big picture in my life until my auntie said to me, "Oh, I feel so sorry for you. The same thing happened to you that happened to your mother. I'm so sorry." When she said the truth, that I've manifested my mother's life completely, that is when the penny dropped for me. Being intellectually aware of something, as opposed to internalising and actually using it is something different. That's when I realised – "Oh my goodness, what the flip have I done?" I don't normally swear. But I did. I did say that. It was fabulous! It was the best thing for me to understand. Because you know what, as soon as I took responsibility for everything showing up in my life was because of me, I was able to change it. So instead of blaming my ex-husband and his girlfriend and everything else and freaking out on him, and saying it's his fault, that he was mean, that he was rude, that he cheated on me. I decided to take full responsibility for everything that was happening in my life. I did this. I was responsible. I manifested everything that was happening outside of me.

Understanding is the first step, but how did I change it? I didn't like my external reality. I didn't like my financial situation. I didn't like where I was. If you don't, how do you change it? That's the question that we will address over the remainder of the chapters in this book. This power lies within every single one of us. Please, if you take only one thing away from this book, take this point: you are responsible for every good, every bad, every ugly, every beautiful thing in your life. This is very important. I have to really push this point. You are responsible. So when you really, fully accept that you are responsible for everything that's happening in your life, you can actually go and change it, you can train your mind to think of things differently. You can train your mind to think "I am now behaving this way." It's sad, but unfortunately most Law of Attraction gurus only focus on this aspect, to think about something good. Always think about something good and good things will show up in your life? That's it? No, it's not! You have to do the internal work; you have some prep to do beforehand.

My life did change dramatically, but it didn't change there and then: I had to go and do the work. And this is where the internal work is - where you have to train your mind to start thinking positively, start thinking about the good things you want. And that is a much harder part than you might realise. Why? Well, imagination has also been called the 'scissors of the mind'. The meaning? Because it's continuously cutting up images in your head. It's like having this huge collage in your mind. If you just imagine this big jumble, and your mind is cutting up all these images that you see in day-to-day life. Now these images, for example, might be from when you're watching TV and disasters happen, murders happen, this bad thing happened or that bad thing happened, even if you're only watching your favourite soap operas, you are internalising and taking pictures. He cheated on her, she cheated on him. This happened, that happened, or you're reading a book or whatever else; it's constantly adding to the collage. As soon as there is some emotion involved in the picture; that image is cut up and plastered on the collage in your internal mind, and sooner or later that image will show up in the external world. That's why your imagination can be called "The scissors of the mind" and you'll become very careful, the more you are aware of this fact, the more careful you will be about the kind of TV you watch, the kind of newspapers you read, the kind of friends you have, the kind of soap operas you watch. My daughter's been watching Jane the Virgin and a few other shows. I watch them with her and I'm able to sit back and watch the social reprogramming that's being done in these programmes. I can pick up on the things happening; the social programming amongst the images, because when you're aware of this, you can say no, and your conscious mind can reject it. I pick up the idea about rich people being bad and money being evil. Therefore, I am able to totally reject it. I can see what they are trying to portray. I am therefore able to vocalise it and say "No! That's wrong." And I vocalise this with my daughter and my daughter picks this up subconsciously and says, "Look, look what they're saying, look how silly that is. Look how silly that point is." I completely negate it. But you have to be aware of what's going in first, be very aware of what's going into your mind because you're constantly picking up ideas. And you're imaging, your imagination is constantly cutting up these images, and plastering them into the collage in your mind, which sooner or later is going to manifest.

Therefore, the point I'm trying to make is that your imagination is super, super powerful, and it's constantly working. Therefore for the remaining chapters, if you can just work with me and do this, so we can start working on reprogramming your subconscious mind together. Be careful of what kind of TV you like, or watching the news. Switch it off, or limit what you watch; I mean, for me, I do trading. I'm into finance. I watch the finance news. I'll keep an eye on what's happening in the finance world. But that's it; I'm working on what's happening with the Forex and so forth and different currencies and the internet. Otherwise, I don't watch much TV. No other news. If I'm watching any soap operas or anything like that, I'm very vigilant, checking what they are trying to say to me subliminally. I just look at it, laugh and then reject it. Look, laugh, reject, look, laugh, reject. And that's it then, it's gone and I'm not considering it.

When it comes to my own reading, I'm also very careful with the kind of material I read. Again; be very vigilant. I watch the kind of company I keep, the people I hang out with, I'm very careful with that. Consider every kind of information you're taking in, because your imagination is cutting out pieces, building that collage of images all the time. That's the important aspect, the place of imagination in your life. Now, let's go on to where and how this imagination plays out, so you know why this is so important.

Why is imagination such a vital part of what's happening in your day to day life? I don't know if you are familiar with this idea, but I divide the mind into three parts; the way I've understood our minds to be, they have three components. There is the subconscious mind, our conscious mind, and finally our super-conscious mind. These three mind sectors are all within you, they're all within me, they reside in each and every one of us; these three separate parts. Some people intermingle these ideas and have interchangeably confused the superconscious with the subconscious, but actually this is not true. I really want to clarify this, that there are three parts to your mind; you have a subconscious mind, you have a conscious mind and you have a super-conscious mind. Let's go into more detail; I'm going to explain to you why your imagination plays a role with all this and how it all fits together. How? By understanding this concept first you can actually then apply these principles and laws to your life.

Your Subconscious Mind

"The subconscious mind is ruled by suggestion, it accepts all suggestions – it does not argue with you – it fulfils your wishes."

Joseph Murphy

What is your subconscious mind? The subconscious mind is simply raw power without direction; think of steam without an engine. It's like electricity, without a grid. It's super powerful, but it doesn't know, or it can't decide what it can do. It just does what it's told to do. It has no power of induction, it doesn't think, it can't justify, it cannot argue with you. It has no arguments at all. It just does what it's told. It's like having a very powerful giant who you can say "Okay, do this" and it'll do it. It doesn't ask, "Honestly, why do you want this? Are you crazy? You don't want this?" It just says, "Okay, you want this? Let me get it for you."

Your Conscious Mind

"The keys to success is to focus our conscious mind on things we desire not things we fear"

Brian Tracy

Now, if you've understood that, let's go on to the second part, which is the conscious mind. So what is the conscious mind? Your conscious mind is actually your human mind. The human mind is responsible for you seeing things, for you to understand things, how you hear, how you listen, how you interact with people, it's actually telling you how life appears to be. It sees death, sickness, disaster, poverty, it sees limitations, it sees how things are - the status quo - and then impresses this onto the subconscious mind. Therefore, when you're watching TV, this is coming into your conscious mind and then being passed over to the subconscious mind. When you're reading, it's going into the conscious mind and it's putting these things into the subconscious. The conscious mind either rejects the information or allows things to go into the subconscious mind. They say that the conscious mind is the doorway to the subconscious mind. In this sense your conscious mind is like a gatekeeper: it decides what to let into the subconscious mind. When I'm watching TV now, my conscious mind is <u>very</u> alert, because it's trained. You need to train your imagination, train your imaging faculty; you have to train your conscious mind to deduce what it will allow into the subconscious mind. So my conscious mind is well trained, in that when I pick up anything negative, once I've looked and laughed, I instantly say "No, no, reject it!" Conversely, if I think of something good using my conscious mind, my subconscious mind will say, "Want this? Okay, let me get it for you." That's it. It's a very powerful tool. It's a very powerful aspect of your mind. But it has no direction - it does what it is told to do. It won't argue with you, it will not laugh at you. Your subconscious mind doesn't have any sense of humour. Think of people who frequently joke about themselves. This is something else to consider. I never say anything derogatory about myself, ever. I look in the mirror, I say; "Oh, Gull you're so beautiful. You're so lovely. I love how you are. You're so healthy. I'm so happy." I'm fasting currently and I'm looking at my energy and feeling energised again. So I'm back to being my normal energetic self, even though I'm fasting. Keep in mind that I haven't had water or food since about one o'clock the previous night. I won't be eating again until nine o'clock this evening, yet I maintain myself as happy and hilarious and funny and whatever else. I was complimenting myself by saying "I love you. You're so wonderful." That's how you need to treat yourself - with love and affection. Because the subconscious mind will accept it, and it will believe it unconditionally. If you tell yourself, "Oh God, I feel so fat," and all you do is laugh at yourself... guess what you're telling your subconscious mind? Remember the subconscious mind doesn't laugh. Your subconscious mind doesn't do humour. Your subconscious mind doesn't have any idea if you're just joking, that you're just messing around. It just says, okay, you're fat. You're dumb. You're stupid. Okay, then. Fine. You see what I mean? Everything that you just laid on yourself, you might say, "it's not a big deal." It IS a big deal. It is. It's so powerful and important for you to understand that this aspect of you, this subconscious part of you is forever listening. This is that part of you that's doing the cutting and pasting into the collage of your mind. So this part of your mind, the subconscious mind, is forever cutting up these images and plastering them on its internal wall. This is the responsibility of your subconscious mind.

Even when watching something stupid and silly, or any of the other programmes that I'm watching with my daughter, my mind is able to deduce "Okay, that's wrong. That's right" and I'm able to verbalise and teach my daughter as we go along with it, and you're able to reject it as you go along, so long as you remain vigilant. Now, when you don't, if you're sitting there like a vegetable and your conscious mind goes into lazy mode, when your conscious mind is not being careful, you are letting in all of these negative images from the news, from the stories, especially when you're angry. When you're in an agitated state, your conscious mind is knocked out; all those negative images are being fed into the subconscious mind, okay? Your conscious mind is responsible for impressing your subconscious mind, giving all these images to your subconscious mind for it to cut up and put on your college.

That's pretty much it - it's tiny, and it doesn't have much power, but it's like the gatekeeper. So it opens the door to your mansion, this huge powerhouse, which is your subconscious mind. But the thing that controls it is your conscious mind. That's the distinction. Now, let's talk about your super-conscious mind.

Your Superconscious mind, your Divine Connection

"The superconscious mind is soul, source, love, the authentic you.
The subconscious mind is what you are.
And the conscious mind is what you do."

Anonymous

The Superconscious is the Divine God mind. Every single person has it. For example, in Hinduism they say, "Namaste," meaning I salute to the Divine in you, that's when they say hello to the Divine in you. Across other religious ideologies they'll say that God is very close to us. In the Old Testament humanity is fashioned in the image of God, and so forth. I think that many religious contexts say this - it is my understanding, you are welcome to take your interpretation of it. My understanding is that all religions are saying the same message, that there's a part of the super conscious, there's a part of the Divine, which is housed in every single individual. Every human, every single human has a bit of Divinity in them, and not just every human, but every single thing. Every part of creation; I mean mountains, I mean trees, I mean everything organic and inorganic. Everyday objects, everything. Everything has Divinity in it, including you – most of all you. The only thing is, with you being here, you have direct communication but you are unaware of it, because until you have trained your intuition, you don't know what's going on. And this is where your intuition comes in.

This intuition part of you is actually your super   conscious, which is connected to Divine Source Energy which is in turn communicating with you. Does this make sense? Your superconscious is the part of your mind connected to Divine Source Energy, which is part of Divinity. This is a part of Divinity which is housed within you, which then communicates your intuition, which then communicates to you to do this and go there, don't go to that house, go to this shop instead. This guy's okay, that woman's not good. This project looks good; this project doesn't look good, and so forth. When you don't listen to your intuition, you always fall flat on your face. If you don't listen to intuition, you make things ten times harder than they need to be. You don't get that desired result, or you feel like you're grinding against something. It's like an uphill struggle against the mountain. This is when you're not listening to intuition.

However, when you DO listen to intuition, it's as if everything falls into place, and you meet the right people at the right time. Things work out. So I'm going to be very clear - I want you to understand this point really, really carefully. This is foundational for you. The superconscious is always present. It's always present. It flashes images in front of you which seem to the conscious, limited mind as unattainable. They're like, "Oh, that's too good to be true. I can't possibly have that!" But you know, it keeps flashing through, so I'm saying this now: <u>you do not have any real desires without the ability to fulfil them.</u>

You do not have a desire, be it acting, writing, or speaking, being a mother, being a father, being a husband, being a daughter, whatever desire you have, whatever relationship, whatever you want from your life, you don't have the desire without the ability, and talent, to attain it. If you want to be a billionaire, if you want to be a rockstar, if you want to be an actor, if you want to be a writer, if you want to be whatever you want to be - **If you have the desire for it, you have the ability to fulfil it.** Because this desire has been placed in there by the superconscious mind.

That's why images flashed through you throughout the day, and throughout your life. They're coming from the super conscious mind. The philosopher Plato talked about Divine design, that every single person has a Divine design. He said there's a Divine design for each person. And it's housed in the super conscious mind. Remember this: for every single person, there is a place that you are to fill, something that you are to do, and something which no one else can do. No one else can do this; it is your Divine design. The Divine Source Energy has designed you for this - has given you a purpose - has given you this particular role. It's there for you, it's there, it's housed in the super conscious mind, now, throughout your life, and this is the responsibility of the super conscious.

To flash those images that tell you, "you need to do this, you need to go here, you need to go do this". And it creates this desire, this inner desire for you to attain it. Now, I'm not saying every single person is able to achieve it, I'm not saying every single person is able to get that desire or is able to get there. What I'm here to say is you have a desire, Divine design, a purpose, a role that you are meant to play. And these images which flash through your mind, into your conscious mind, every now and again, is your super-conscious mind, which is the Divine Mind talking to you - telling you, you need to get here, you need to do this, this is what you need to get, and that *creates the desire* within you. For example, for me, it's money.

I became this expert, I have to say hand on heart I am the best person I know when it comes to talking about money. Why? Because I had the desire for it. I had such a massive desire to learn everything related to money, how to clear your ideas and your energy around money, how to train your imagination, how to train your imaging faculty around money, how to do it, that was my desire. And it was flashed into my brain through my conscious mind by the superconscious.

My super-conscious told me I can attain it; God's Divine Energy does not give you any desire without the ability to attain it. And this is why the super-conscious actually gives you those desires, so you can have this, and you can have that. And then it's your responsibility to pick it up and recognise those desires as God's way of communicating to you what is already in the Universal warehouse destined for you. And it's constantly happening.

So it's not like Divine Source Energy just gives you the desire and then walks away... because the super-conscious is part of you. It's housing intuition. It gives you that intuitive guidance. Do this, meet this person, go ahead and do that, hence our intuition is speaking to us all the time, irrespective of whether we listen or not. We are guided throughout our life to go and do certain tasks, to attain success, to cultivate our hidden talents (even those unknown to us) to meet certain individuals and attain all those material things. Am I making sense? Am I explaining this clearly? I want you to understand this. I don't know anybody else who is talking about these three different components of your mind; your conscious, your subconscious, and superconscious. The Divine Source Energy is connected to your super-conscious which is housed inside YOU. And this is so important for you to understand. This is why every single person has intuition, and I mean every single person, even those who are not listening and therefore think they don't have intuition. Yes my intuition might be more trained than yours, but it doesn't mean that I have more intuition than you, I simply use it more - see? Because we have the same super conscious mind within ourselves, you too can train yourself to listen to intuition better, but we both have the same potential intuitive powers. This is a very important distinction to understand.

Now that we've clarified the three minds, we can go on to talking about what it is, how we can clarify our understanding of it, and how we can train our imaging mind. The problem that we have at the moment is the *nature* of most of the images which are going into your collage and are plastered in your subconscious mind. Remember the subconscious is responsible for bringing everything in. So you have your subconscious mind, you have your conscious mind and your super-conscious - your intuition telling your conscious mind what you desire, what you should be getting. The conscious mind is responsible for feeding information into the subconscious mind. And the subconscious mind is a super powerhouse which makes sure that whatever you have outside matches with whatever's inside, so everything that's happening outside of you is made up by your subconscious mind.

Therefore if your subconscious decides you should have this health problem or this worrying issue, it's your subconscious mind that decides this is the problem we have at the moment. And this is what I made my life mission to solve - that most of the subconscious is programmed to think in a certain way. It's programmed - so if your subconscious mind is programmed to see things in a different way, and it tells the conscious mind to look for those things, then you'll look for those things. It's not as easy as saying that the conscious mind is the master of the subconscious mind. The problem is when you're going from zero to seven years old; your conscious mind is a baby. It's not there yet. So, guess what happens? You pick up the beliefs and paradigms from those around you, especially your primary care givers. Therefore, you have eighty percent of your subconscious programming done FOR YOU by your primary caregivers by the time you are seven. Between seven and eight, your conscious mind fully develops and starts to form the idea of "ME, Myself and I". Thereby becoming the gatekeeper for the subconscious mind. However, as the conscious mind only follows what it has learned over the early years, it continues to provide the subconscious mind with things, images and beliefs that are SIMILAR to what it received before it was fully formed.

The training that the subconscious mind gets in how to look, what to look for, and how to see things has been given to the conscious mind by the subconscious mind. Am I making this clear? This is profound information. Most people don't understand this concept. Your subconscious mind, after the age of seven, has a gatekeeper which is a conscious mind. But the conscious mind up into that point has been trained by the subconscious to look for things. So if you think people are bad then people will be bad. If you think the world's out to get you then the world's out to get you. If you think money is scarce, then money is scarce. If you think money is hard to come by then money's hard to come by, because your subconscious mind has been trained to look for these things. A simple example, a quick experiment even, is to look around the room quickly and take in everything that's GREEN. Okay, now you've done that close your eyes, and then look again.

So the first time, you'll see one or two things are green, but upon the second time around, you'll actually see many more green things, don't you? Because your conscious mind has been trained up until the age of seven, to look for things in a certain way. This means from that point onwards, if it's trained to see life as hard, if it's trained to see the money's hard to come by, if it's trained to see that people are horrible, people are too harsh and people treat you badly, that is what the conscious mind will look for, and that's what the conscious mind will find. The conscious mind finds things to reinforce the beliefs and especially the paradigms installed in the subconscious programming.

Now, this is the catch twenty-two situation: what do we do first? Do we work on the conscious mind or do we work on the subconscious? Most people try to do it backwards. They say, "Oh, okay, I need to think positively. Let me work on my conscious mind. If the conscious mind is the gatekeeper for the subconscious, if I just change my conscious mind, if I use my willpower, I can decide what my subconscious mind will make." Now using your willpower to change your conscious mind is hard. Imagine it this way in fact; your subconscious mind is like a massive aeroplane.

And your conscious mind is the pilot. If you're changing ideas and thinking; if I change my pilot's way of thinking, my subconscious mind will be fine, then you are going to make life really difficult. And that's why the Law of Attraction hasn't worked in your favour until now; I'm giving you the real reason here. What you need to do is work on <u>both</u> - you have to work on your pilot, you have to change what the poor pilot has been thinking about, all those wrong things, the lack and limitation. So you have to change your thinking. That's where you can use willpower. So that includes your vision boards and your intention statements and everything else. That's the affirmations that work on your conscious mind. Now we have to simultaneously work on your subconscious mind. This is where you have to use energy tools. Now I have found there are various tools out there, Psychic K, there's EFT, many various modalities of energy healings. I use my own personal modality, which is where I use my voice, my tone of voice, where I use my words, and I use my intention and my personal energy because I'm very, very clear. I use all of that in totality as one modality to clear your energy and we clear your subconscious mind. Now I'm not saying you have to come and work with me. It's up to you - not everyone will be ready to work with me, it's perfectly fine.

I'm not saying everybody should come in and enjoy my energy clearings - you do what resonates with you. My energy clearings are very particular. Because I do use my voice, I use my tonality; I use the speed of my voice. One of the things that until now I didn't know why I had, I can speak extremely fast and I wasn't sure why as I've always tried to slow down. That is one of my superpowers that I use as part of my modality, as an energy tool - it's a tool for me to clear your energy. Now, it may not work with you specifically so you may have to find an alternative, but many people find my energy tools work very powerfully and effectively for them. There are so many things out there: EFT, Psychic K, Reiki, different types of music, Ho'o Pono Pono, I use Ho'o Pono Pono myself and with my clients but there are so many different modalities out there that you can use, but you have to do this - you have to work simultaneously on both your subconscious and your conscious mind. Remember the superconscious is just responsible for giving you the desire and housing your intuition. If you understand how the mind works then you'll be able to start working out for yourself - what am I supposed to do? What do I want?

The first thing you need to decide is what you want, and then if you train your pilot - your conscious mind - you know through affirmations, through vision boards and through being very disciplined, that's where willpower comes in along with your subconscious mind. That's when you train your mind but you have to clear your subconscious programming. Now majority of the subconscious programming is usually done between age zero and seven. And this is where most people get stuck. This is what people need my energy clearing services for.

There are several different modalities, you're welcome to explore all of them and find whatever works with you. If my voice resonates with you, if my energy resonates with you, and then come work with me. If it doesn't, if it's not something that you resonate with, you'll know. (The best way to know if my energy tools will work for you is by joining one of my Workshops. You can look for the next upcoming workshop here: https://www.abundancemindsetmakeover.com/workshop.) Your intuition will tell you which people to work with. I've explained my energy healings, why they work so well because people get phenomenal results. For example, take my client Martini. She recently shared with the my Mastermind group that the day after we did a manifestation call, I think she wanted to manifest $7,000, the very next day, within 24 hours, she manifested $7,000.

Now the reason why this works is, my energy clearings open up your subconscious mind, we can just take out the old limiting beliefs energetically and drop in the new high vibrational belief to replace the old one.

I take out all the energy which is rubbish, which is old energy, and we drop in the new energy and it integrates with your subconscious mind. That's how my energy clearings work, if that helps you to understand the concept. You're welcome to explore and if mine works for you then come to me. If not, you will find what you feel does work.

Prayer a powerful way to Manifest!

"True prayer is neither a mere mental exercise nor a vocal performance. It is far deeper than that - it is a spiritual transaction with the Creator of Heaven and Earth."

Charles Spurgeon

Think of the act of prayer. Prayer is when you're talking to Divine Source Energy. Prayer is when you're using your conscious mind, you're emotionalising it because when you pray to Divine Source Energy, you pray with emotion. If you're just praying to God, "give me this God, give me that", it doesn't really work. The reason why prayers are so powerful is because when you start believing that you're talking to your God, you're talking to your Divine Source Energy, you're talking to the Supreme Being, you are then using your conscious mind to connect to the Supreme Being, via the power of the super conscious. Divine Source Energy is always connected to you through your super conscious, it's always connected to you so it can hear you

- it can listen to what you're saying. It can constantly hear what you're saying, and what you're doing. Does that make sense?

When you pray, you're using imagination, you're emotionalising it and you're verbalising it even if you don't speak out loud, even if you're only speaking internally. You're also verbalising what you want, you're imaging what you want, and you're speaking with emotion. That's why prayers are so powerful. That's why people say their prayers have been answered. That's the best way to manifest. How do I personally manifest? I pray, I pray to Divine Source Energy, I go on my Prayer mat and do my salah (prayer), and my head is on the floor. And you know, in the prayer stage, I'm praying, and that's my form of manifestation, for me personally, because when I speak to the Divine, I am connected, I am crying, I am emotional. You cannot get more emotional than when you are in this devout state where you might say, "God, I love you. Thank you. Thank you, thank you," and you have tears coming down your face. You are in a state of gratitude to the Divine for everything you have. And you say, "Thank you for this, and I love you so much. thank you for all the good that is coming to me, I'm so thankful for this. And I know you're going to give me (my desire) also". Because in your state of expectation, you're saying "God, I love you for everything you give me. And I know you're going to give me this too" and you are therefore stating an expectation. What does the Law of Attraction say? Imagine what you want, ask for it. Ask for it in a way that's positive, and then emotionalise it and hold expectations for it. When you do prayer, you do all of those things simultaneously without even thinking... because you're talking to a Supreme Being and thinking, "Thank you God, thank you. Thank you for everything you've given me. I know this is amazing. You've given me so much and I know the next thing is you're going to give me that too because you are so awesome". And then if you can, if you cry about it as I do when I pray, especially when I'm fasting because when you fast spiritually you elevate yourself and you get that closer connection with Divine Source Energy - I really believe that during Ramadan my power of manifestation increases by manifold. I think that's probably why the last manifestation was so powerful for Martini; honest and truthful shows of emotion bring you closer to God. Prayers are that powerful because you are using your conscious mind. It is where you are emotionalising, you are putting in all the essential ingredients for a powerful manifestation. And that's why prayers work so well.

Now another quote, and this is off on a bit of a tangent, but I'm going to tell you that Collective Consciousness; where people have prayed together, this is why those prayers work so much. Because when you have two or more people together, focusing their minds on a collective goal, things happen more powerfully. This is why when people pray together, your manifestations are that much quicker. That's why our Manifestation Calls are so powerful, because it's not just me. It's my clients, collectively as a group, we are manifesting for each other as well as ourselves. And that's why they work so beautifully. That's why the manifestations are super powerful, and people get results in such an amazing way, be it if they attend my mastermind sessions personally, or even by just applying what they learn and take away from my teachings, such as you are from this book.

This brings us to the end of this chapter. I hope you enjoyed it - this was foundational work, it's essential for you to understand and know before we go on to the other parts and the actual Laws. So this is for you to understand. And then the Laws are for you to apply the principles in your life and run with it. And every single principle, every single Law of Prosperity is a powerful law.

Quick Recap.

I hope you enjoyed this chapter. I hope you thought it was as amazing as I think it is. These principles are powerful. I'm going to quickly do a recap. Remember, your imagination is your superpower; it's something that you have that no other animal does. That makes you special - that makes you human. This makes you closer to God. We also talked about how training your imaging faculty is really important. And before you can train the imaging faculty, you have to understand the three components of your mind which are the subconscious, the conscious and the super-conscious mind. These initial concepts will help you understand all the knowledge to come.

Chapter 2

YOUR MONEY AVATAR

*"Money does not buy you happiness, but lack of money
certainly buys you misery."*

— **Daniel Kahneman**

In this chapter, we're going to talk about your Money Avatar. What is it? What do you do with it? How does it help you with your money? Let's find out!

What does your money avatar look like? Is it a he or a she? And why is it so important? Before we actually talk about Money Avatars, what they are, and how to find what your money avatar is, let's discuss why it is so important.

Now, as in the previous chapter, I've talked about the fact that most people have this really negative relationship with money. Consciously, they may be saying, "I want money. I like money. I want to have more money in my life." But subconsciously, they have these really negative feelings, and ideas, about money. Therefore, here is an exercise we can do –get a pen and paper, to really write out how you feel about money and get all your emotions about money on paper. I suggest you put a timer on your phone for 5 minutes, and then start writing about money. Aim to constantly write for the duration of the entire 5 minutes. You should not lift the pen, and you will find at one point, the subconscious mind takes over and starts to put things on there that your conscious mind was not even aware of. This is a very powerful exercise. Please do it now. Come back to the book after this exercise. I hope you did the exercise. What's the first thing that comes to mind when you think about money? I promise you, most people, if they're honest and they're struggling with money, the first thing that comes to their mind is bills, mortgages, rent, credit cards, hire car purchase bills, whatever else that hangs over them like a dismal, financial cloud. Everything that's related to money going out, which causes them to feel stress and frustration and anger towards money. You'd be surprised how you will actually blame money for the lack of it. "I just can't have money," or, "What the hell do I need money for? Money's so annoying. Money's so this," etc, etc, fill in the blanks.

Whereas, in truth, money has nothing to do with it. It's not money's fault that you are not attracting it. It's not money's fault that you are repelling it. It's not money's fault that it's not coming close to you. This is why this chapter is so important. I want you to actually verbalise or write it down. When you think of money, what comes to your mind? Is it bills? Is it student loans? Is it credit card bills? Once you have an idea of everything that comes to your mind when thinking about money, how does it make you feel?

If we're being honest; most people don't feel great when they're paying the rent, the mortgage, or credit cards. If anything, they feel negatively. They say, "Do I have enough to cover all the bills? Do I have enough to make sure I meet all my needs? All my demands?"

That's the first thing that most people think about. "Do I have enough in the bank to make sure that everything's paid this month?" I remember it well because I used to be one of them. I'm not much different from you reading right now. I'm the 2.0 version of you. I had these same thoughts go through my mind and this is irrespective of the amount of money you make. I find, because most of my clients are from professional backgrounds, and being a lawyer, I attract a lot of them, like doctors, lawyers, and accountants. I attract a lot of those as clients, as well as entrepreneurs and a few business owners. That negative thinking always appears as a pattern in most of them.

I remember having this conversation with a doctor one time. She was a doctor, and her husband is an IT specialist. Their combined income was around one hundred and fifty thousand pounds a year annually, which is quite a lot for anybody. Yet, we were having the discussion because she was worried about making ends meet because the financial commitments they held were too much, and they were really struggling financially. Now, how does someone struggle with money when they're bringing that much in annually?

This is where I come in, because this is where I can bring a spotlight into your life. This is why, regardless of how much money is coming in, money's never going to be enough to satisfy you if you don't understand the 'nature' of money. The first step for you to understand this starts with you being very honest with yourself and asking yourself, "Okay, what do I normally think about when I think about money?" Not what you're told in the books. Not what you're consciously thinking, not what "The science of getting rich" tells me that I have to love it. We need to be more positive in our thinking about money. Be honest with yourself. What's your day-to-day thinking about money? When you generally hear the word "money", what is it that comes to your mind? Not enough? Will I have enough to pay the bills, etc? That's always the first thing with most people, and that's the first mistake right there.

Now, if you're answering this and if you understand the Law of Attraction, the Law of Attraction says that you need to have positive and loving emotions for whatever you want to attract. Otherwise, you repel it. That includes money, the same as anything else. If you need to feel positive and happy towards money in order to attract it, the question is DO YOU feel happy and positive towards money?

I'll go through, in later chapters, how to remove blocks and what kind of blocks are preventing you, but generally as an overarching idea, how do we get to feel positive about money? The answer lies in actually becoming friends with money. Now, I don't know about you, but I find it very difficult to become friends with inanimate objects.

Actually, that's probably not as true for now because I'm friends with a lot of organic matter like trees and plants; but a piece of paper? Paper, in general, or coins, lumps of precious metal; it's very difficult to bring emotions up towards these things. Because you don't. You may use money to buy a better lifestyle, a better car, have better food, etc, but that doesn't actually make you have the affiliation and love and respect for those coins and pieces of paper.

This is the idea that I had, going back a few years ago when my idea of the Money Avatar was born. Now, we know for a fact that quantum physics teaches that everything is energy. Quantum physics teaches at its core that everything is just lots of molecules circling each other. Within the molecules are atoms, and within the atoms there are electrons and neutrons; and in the centre, at the core, everything is energy, which includes money too.

If everything is energy, but money is in the non-physical plane, where you can't see it with the naked eye, then why do I need to see money as piece of paper? This is where the Money Avatar was born. I want you to actually personify money. I want you to have an image of money. This could be anyone, someone similar (but NOT actually) a movie star, an author. It could be an old, wise person. It could be someone from the past, the present, or from the future. It doesn't really matter. This is personal to you. Everyone's Money Avatar will be different. But I want you to personify it. I don't want you to have an inanimate object. I want you to have a living creature.

Now people ask, whether they can use animals as their money avatar? If you're really close to animals, rather than humans, you can use an animal as your money avatar. You can use a tiger, a dog, a cat, etc, as your money avatar. That's possible. However, I want you to use living creatures ONLY. Ideally, I want you to personify money into human form. I know there are people who love animals more, and if that's you then personify it as a particular animal that you really love and care for. Personally, I like a human Money Avatar.

The first step is to actually make this Money Avatar in the non-physical form as a person (or an animal). Then, get their personality. For example, my Money Avatar is called Michelle and she is this sexy, sassy, amazing woman. I get goosebumps when I talk about her because she's my best friend. This is an amazing woman who's funny as hell. She can be a bit of a bimbo, she can do funny things and she has a great sense of humour. She can be a bit silly like me and she loves everything, she loves Bollywood. She's a Greek goddess. In my mind, she has these golden locks and she wears a toga and she's funny as hell and incredibly intelligent.

That's my Money Avatar. She's funny, she's witty and she's always got my back.

When you personify money, that's your Money Avatar. Once you have yours, you can then give it personality characteristics. How do they behave? What do they do? But the most important characteristic they must have is that they are your best friend, they always have your back. Can you see why we just did that? In a matter of seconds, we've actually created an environment where you can start developing a positive, healthy relationship with money. This is absolutely crucial. What you don't want is greed for money. What you don't want is the "need" for money. Being a banking and finance lawyer, and being an advocate in general, I would say I'm on the planet as an advocate for money. I really do feel that. Maybe that's more true to what I am.

As an advocate for money, I can say that in order for you to have more money in your life, you need to have a better relationship with it. The best way to create a relationship with someone is to become friends with them. When you're friends with somebody, you don't need them. You don't want to hold on to them. You don't want to put them in a cage somewhere. You don't want to lock them in a room somewhere. You want to have fun with this person. You want to have fun with your best friend. You also know that your best friend will be there before you know you need it. Your best friend will be telepathic and think, "Oh yeah, Gull's upset. Let me go and see what's up". Then they turn up at your doorstep and ask "What's up with you? I was thinking about you and just felt like I needed to call on you."

Your friends have this telepathic connection with you, this emotional connection. If you're down, if you need them, they'll turn up. That's what friends do. And that's the kind of relationship we want to create with money. You want money to become your best friend who turns up even before you realise you need them. This is the idea of your Money Avatar - somebody who's going to have your back, who's always going to support you as they come and go. Now, this is so important for you to understand. There's an ebb and flow to money. Money will come. Money will go. When it comes to you, it has to go somewhere else. It has to go somewhere else because that's part of its journey. That's the ebb and flow of money. If you try to hold onto it too tightly, you find it eventually slips out your hand, like grains of sand falling through your fingers.

On the other hand, if you allow money to have this flow, to come and go and be happy, when you receive money and you're then happy for it to go because you know it's going to come back, this is when money starts coming in larger abundance. This is the idea of your best friend. Your best friend would come to you, spend some time with you, spend a lot of time with you even and have lots of fun with you, but then go on their merry way and do whatever it needs to. But you will be fine. The stronger the relationship you build with money, the more often you see your best friend. If you really enjoy someone's company, you find that you're spending more time with them. You're going out with them, maybe going bowling or to lunch or dinner, etc. You spend more and more time with your best friend because you enjoy each other's company. You make time for him or her because you enjoy and respect that closeness, that relationship that you want to continue throughout your life.

That's the idea with money. Money will continue to come and go from your energy field, yet it might not be stuck in your bank account or in any particular place. If you allow it to come and go, to flow and do it with ease and grace, enjoy it with happiness, then you're happy to receive money and also happy for it to leave. Obviously, you know your friend is going to come back with the expectation that you're going to see each other again in a bit. You're going to see your best friend shortly, and with the expectation that you're going to meet them again, you let them go.

This is absolutely crucial that we need to have that kind of relationship with money because money will need to come and money will need to go. Do you see what I mean? Do you see how powerful this is? Now a question I regularly get is "Well, what does my Money Avatar look like? I'm blank, how do I come up with one?" I would say that if you are really blank and you really can't decide how to come up with your Money Avatar, then sit down and think, "Okay, what would your best friend look like?" You probably have a best friend at the moment, but if you had your ideal best friend, what would he or she look like? Would it be a man? Would it be a woman? Or would it be an animal? Then, give them a name. What would they like? What would their interests be? How would they behave? How would they interact with you? How would you know that they are your best friend?

Write it down. Sit down and work out who would be your ideal best friend? Give them a name and that's your Money Avatar. Now, keep in mind, as you evolve, as you continue to read this book, and you continue to move forward at learning and going through my programmes, you'll find that your ideas and beliefs and thoughts around money begin to change. Then, you'll also find your Money Avatar evolves too. That's perfectly fine - why would your best friend stay the same? Your best friend wouldn't. They would evolve and grow too, just as you would evolve and grow. Expect your Money Avatar to grow with you and then your relationship with money will change. It will become more solid and defined. That's perfectly fine and that's what we're after. We're not after a static relationship. We want this to be a dynamic relationship. One that grows and evolves over time. This is extremely important.

Let's recap:

To recap, we've talked about your Money Avatar and the importance of having or creating one. The first thing that you need to do is ask yourself what is your current ideology, your thinking, your feelings about money and just be very honest with yourself. When money pops into your mind, what are the thoughts that run through your head? Credit card bills, mortgage, student loans, et cetera? Then, when you think about those bills, how do you feel? Do you feel happy or sad? Most people feel frustration and anger. If nothing else, it's stressful to think, "Okay, do I have enough to cover all my bills?" This stress is one of the major issues. Well, what does stress do? It releases cortisol in your body and it causes you to feel bad. Not good, at all.

The second step is to create a Money Avatar. How do we create a Money Avatar? Sit down; write down the characteristics of your best friend. Would it be a man, woman or an animal? Give them a name. How would they behave? What kind of personality would they have and how would you interact? Then, after you've done this, you need to sit down and talk to your Money Avatar every single day to build a relationship. This happens quite a lot in our workshops. I talk about this quite extensively in my Abundance Mindset Makeover Workshop which by the way, you get to hear about a lot in this book. I suggest you do register. Here is the link to register

https://www.abundancemindsetmakeover.com/workshop We do these three, sometimes four times a year. During these workshop I talk about your Money Avatar and we go in-depth extensively in terms of how to connect with your Money Avatar and what to do about it. Then, I take you through a meditation in terms of connecting with your money and the energy of money. But the point is you need to be able to feel really connected to your Money Avatar. Then, maybe the first time you meet them, it may be a very standoffish relationship. You may be setting up a meeting.

You can barely say hello, or they don't look upon you or you're unable to interact with them. Because you're meeting with this complete stranger. For most people, this is probably the first time you actually decided to meet your money in the spiritual world, in this format. Normally, you're used to seeing money as pieces of paper or coins or gold and silver. But you're not used to seeing money as this personification, which is the Money Avatar – specifically YOUR Money Avatar.

If this is the first time you meet them, as when you first start meeting strangers yourself, you may not have a happy relationship. You may not hit it off really quickly. There are other times when you meet strangers and you think "Oh my Goodness, you're amazing. You're my best friend. I love you to bits." That can happen too. But there are times, depending on how you've treated money subconsciously all of these years; money may not be so open to you. Money may not want to build a relationship with you. It's quite normal. So give it time and patience and build that relationship with money over time.

Once you've decided what your Money Avatar is, then it is time for you to sit down, meditate, talk and speak to them and get to know his or her needs and desires from you. Remember, it's a two-way communication. When your best friends can tell you, "Well, you know what, Gull, I need you to do X, Y and Z." You say, "Yeah, that's fine. Absolutely fine, Michelle. Okay, let's get X, Y and Z done." Then you can say, "Michelle, do you mind coming over, helping me out here? I need some help." It's a two-way relationship. You both give, and receive, from each other. That's what best friends are for. You've got each other's back. The best gift that your Money Avatar will give you is that you will begin to trust and believe that money has your back. That money will show up for you easily and effortlessly, and that money's always there for you. This is so, so important.

I hope you enjoyed this chapter. The Money Avatar is one of my favourite topics to talk about because I don't think people realise how powerful this one concept is in terms of building a healthy relationship with money. Think about it, with your best friend, you don't think, "Oh, please, please, please come around. I really miss you." If you do that to anybody, they'll feel suffocated and they'll run away from you. On the other hand, if you pick up the phone and say, "Michelle, I am really missing you, girl.

Come on, let's have lunch together. Let's go for a coffee or drinks together." Your friend would say "Yeah, sure. Let's go meet up." You'll meet up and then have an amazing time. This is the difference between wanting and being greedy and needy for money. This way, we have a healthy relationship with money. We have love and respect for it. I want you to NOT have need or greed for money. I want you to have a healthy relationship with money and to have respect and love for it.

Do you see the difference? I hope you will now go and create your money avatar. I'll see you in the next chapter!

THE FIRST LAW OF MONEY – THE LAW OF THE WORD

"Words are free. It's how you use them that may cost you."

— **KushandWizdom**

W elcome to chapter three of The Laws of Money. We are talking about the first Law of Money, the Law of words.

However, be first of all, I just want to make sure we're on the same page, I'm going to cover a few principles of the Law of Attraction, and then I'm going to go into the details of energy. You know; what energy is, and I'm going to explain a little bit further. And then I'm going to talk about the power of thoughts, I'm going to talk about the power of words, why words are more powerful than thoughts, and then I'm going to explain to you the dangers of jokes. What? What could be wrong with joking? Why would you not joke around? What could possibly be wrong with that? Well, self-deprecating jokes, and self-deprecating humour is quite dangerous. So I'm going to explain the dangers of that too. And then, of course, I'll give you the way forward, as always.

The Three Core Principles behind the Law of Attraction.

There are three principles for the Law of Attraction, which you may already know but I want to make sure we everyone is clear about them. The first principle is that everything is energy: you, your hair, your eyes, your thoughts, your words, your phone, everything is energy. That's the first principle.

Principle number two, if everything is energy, everything is therefore vibrating at a particular frequency. And depending on the frequency, you either see it as a solid, liquid, or you don't see it at all. So it may be something invisible to the naked eye.

Principle number three is you attract to yourself whatever you're in harmony with, or in alignment with.

So those are the three principles of the Law of Attraction, if you've not covered them before, and I just wanted to reiterate them, before I talk about energy.

What does it mean to say that everything is Energy?

There are Nobel Prize awardees in physics that have proven beyond a reasonable doubt that the physical world is nothing but an ocean of energy. It materialises and it dematerialises over and over and over again. Nothing is actually solid, there is no such thing as solid matter. The fact that we think something is solid is actually only our perception of it, but it's just an illusion. Not the reality. The reality is it is purely energy.

Now I am going to talk a bit about this, and I want to cover a little bit of Quantum Physics. This is not supposed to be a Quantum Physics lesson, but I want you to understand the principles. I want you to approach this aspect of the Law of Attraction from a scientific point of view. I am a scientist at heart. I'm also a mathematician. They are all the workings, the machinery, of Divine Source Energy.

So for me I need a logical explanation. This is what I want to give you a little bit of insight into Quantum Physics, so that you understand why what I'm about to tell you works and why it's absolutely imperative that you follow the instructions as I give them to you.

So let's get into this. This is the world of quantum physics where nothing is solid. And the atoms are all the time materialising and dematerialising at every split second in time. Now these scientists have proven that thoughts, be they yours or mine, are responsible for holding the ever-changing fields of energy together in the form, and the shape, of the object as we see it. For example, if you pick up your phone, it's my thoughts and your thoughts which are making it into a phone as we see it - that's the simplified idea behind it.

Now, we have five senses: we have sight, hearing, touch, smell and taste. And each of these senses has a specific range, so our vision has a particular range; our hearing has a particular range. For instance, we know dogs can hear more that we can. And animals can see a lot further across the visible spectrum than we can. Snakes have a completely different spectrum altogether, compared to how we see light and colour. So our senses perceive energy within certain fixed parameters - that's the first thing to understand.

And once we pick those energies up within those parameters, they are interpreted by our brain, which again, is another form of energy, and it's given to us as a form of perception.

Therefore, nothing is either exact or complete. It's just our perception of how things are. Now, if this is the first time you heard about this concept from Quantum Physics, I know it's a bit difficult to get your head around. But I just want you to understand it. Basically Quantum Physics is saying that things are the way they are, not because they are the way they are, but because of your understanding and your expectation of it to be that way. Take a moment to just get your head around that. All of our interpretations are based exclusively on a map of what we think is actually reality. And I could keep talking about it, and this is why your inner world dictates your external world. I'm going to repeat that; your inner world dictates your external world. What we've always seen is actually based on what we believe we'll see or what we believe our inner map to be, what we believe our inner world to be, and therefore, our outer world is actually <u>not real</u>. It's just our understanding of the energy. And that's reflected out. It's a bit much to get your head around at first, but this is the way it is.

Our map is built as a result of the collective experiences of our personal lives, and those of our ancestors, because now it's also been proven that DNA contains memories. It's called Epigenetics.

Epigenetics is a field of science which talks about how DNA carries over memories from your ancestors. What all of this means is that your idea of how this world works, or how things are working, is based not only on your personal life experiences, but those of your ancestors as well. If this is a bit confusing, just stay with me, I promise you, I will simplify it for you. I just want to give you some groundwork

44

on Quantum Physics, that's all. So everything you see in the physical world, in basic terms all started off as a thought. Imagine a phone for example, the phone case, the phone itself, initially it was just a thought, and then it was brought into the physical world. Therefore, you literally turn your thoughts into reality, and into physical objects. And therefore, your life becomes what you imagined, and what you believe it to be.

Literally, the exterior world is mirroring the internal world. It therefore allows you to experience everything you believe to be true in your three-dimensional world. So the only way to change your external world is to change your internal world.

Now, Quantum Physics tells us that the world is not constant, as it may appear to be. Instead, it's a place of constant motion: you're constantly moving, things are constantly changing, and our individual and collective thoughts keep building and tearing down and rebuilding these objects and the images into the 'reality'. I'll repeat this point, it's that important - Your thoughts are actually the ones, collectively and individually, that are building, tearing down and rebuilding the images or the objects you see before you, okay? It's perpetually mobile, constantly moving. In this sense we're just lighting the most beautiful and intelligent configuration. And energy is constantly changing under the surface. And all that's controlled via powerful thoughts. This energy is changing all the time, and the one thing that is controlling it is your mind. Remember, we covered the mind as the foundational work with the three components of our mind being defined as the subconscious, the conscious and the super-conscious.

So you're this powerful human being. But if you were to look at yourself under a strong electromagnetic microscope, you'd see that you are made up of clusters, forever changing energy in the shapes of electrons, neutrons, photons, and subatomic particles, simple as that. Everything, you and everything else around you, as proven by Quantum Physics, is created by the act of observing the object. And, therefore, when you observe an object, you determine how it reacts. So depending on how you're viewing the particle, and what you expect the particle to behave as, that's how the particle behaves.

This is literally, in Quantum Physics terms, what we're talking about. The object does not exist independently of its observer. So the particles do not exist independently. And as you see things as you observe things, that's how things are happening.

I hope I haven't just confused you. I have tried to keep it simple - Quantum Physics is something that I love talking about, but I hope I made it easy to comprehend. I want you to understand why energy is so important. That's why I wanted to cover Quantum Physics briefly. I literally just covered two years' worth of study in about five minutes, but hopefully I didn't confuse you too much. Let's move on now.

Three Components of You, Your Mind, Body, Soul

"The body is an outstanding source of strength; the mind an incredible source of intelligence; the heart an uncommon source of might; and the soul a remarkable source of power."
— **Anonymous.**

Let's talk about the three components of you. So what are you, what are the three components? Your world consists of your soul, your mind, and your body; those are the three parts that make up who you are.

Each of these three has a function that is quite unique. What you can see with your own eyes, and experience with your own body is the physical world. The body is in effect created by thoughts, and therefore it has no meaning itself. You are a physical being at the moment - you have your senses, your eyes, your ears, etc, all of those make up your body. Now, the cause is thought - your thoughts define how your body is shaped, how it is, whether you're healthy, unhealthy, what happens in your life, whatever else. So that's basically taking personal responsibility to the next level. We're saying, on a quantum physics level, that you are responsible for every aspect of yourself. If you understand this point, that thoughts are really powerful, then you understand that your thoughts are pretty much creating you and breaking you and recreating you again, that's what we're saying, (that's why thoughts are so powerful). The body cannot produce, it can only experience and be experienced, and that's its unique ability.

On the other hand, thoughts cannot experience. Think of it this way; thoughts cannot experience alone, they can only experience through the body and the body can't do anything by itself because it needs the thoughts. Thus, thoughts can only make, create and interpret, they cannot experience, just as the body cannot think or create, it can only experience. So that's the relationship between your thoughts, your mind and your body.

Your mind needs a world of relativity and the physical, i.e. the body, to be experienced by the mind, that's why your mind needs your body. This is the connection between the mind and the body. Your mind cannot experience things physically, that's where it needs a body, but the body cannot think for itself, it needs the mind. Your body actually needs the mind and the mind needs a body. This symbiosis is the first thing to remember.

Okay, so that's the connection between the mind and the body, but where does the soul come in? The soul is the one that gives the thought to the body and the mind. So your soul is what combines your mind and body. It's like the glue which connects your body to your mind, and it makes you complete as the person who you are. As soon as the soul leaves, you die and you're in the ground, the body loses connection with the mind and you're done. This is an important thing to understand because the soul is neither the mind nor the body, it combines these two together, it glues the whole thing together and it holds everything in one place. The body has no power to create, although it gives the illusion that it does. That's something really important to understand - the body cannot do anything but help you to experience life. So I always say this: you are a spiritual being, i.e. you are this Divine Being having this physical experience, and you have this physical experience through your body.

Maybe it sounds a little woo woo but just bear with me and humour me for now. Your body is there for you to experience this physical life. So, within respectful levels of reason you shouldn't be abstaining from physical pleasures unless it's for important reasons. I think we're here to experience life in its full glory. If you want to travel, if you want to enjoy good food, it's your prerogative to choose to live how you want to. You should experience everything in its magnificent form. Which includes love and affection and emotion.

The body is pure effect and has no power to cause or create. It doesn't have any thinking ability, only the mind can think and only the body can experience. If you understand this now, the bottom line is your thoughts are creating – that's the first Law which I think you've heard time and time again, from many experts not just myself. Most people who talk about the Law of Attraction talk about this, about how thoughts are really important. Thoughts become things; thinking brings thoughts alive through energy and vibration, and so forth. I always talk about the fact that you're sending thoughts out into the Universe. So thoughts are really important. The more powerful your thoughts are, the more your thoughts are responsible for you. Your thoughts are responsible for creating your reality; your thoughts are responsible for creating your world.

Now, what is even more important than your thoughts, are your words. So the very first Law states that it's through words that you can change your thoughts, you can use your willpower to change your thoughts. This is super powerful for you to understand. That your thoughts are powerful. Yes, they are. But what's more powerful are your words. You can use your words to change your thoughts, because remember, thoughts are subconscious and subconsciously you're thinking all the time anyway. How do you change your thoughts? Through the power of words. The reason is because your words become your laws. This is so powerful. Your words become your laws. For example, when I say "I'm always late," guess what? I'm now forever late.

It doesn't matter how hard I try, I'm always going to be late. If I said, "I keep losing my patience with my children. I don't know why I keep losing my patience with my children." Guess what? It doesn't matter how hard I try to be patient, I will lose patience with my children. "Oh, I just missed the bus, every single time, I don't know what it is, I just missed the bus like I always do." Again, it doesn't matter how early I leave my home, I will still always miss the bus. Because if nothing else, something else will happen. My neighbour will come out and distract me, something will happen which makes sure that I will miss the bus and hence; you will always miss the bus.

Therefore your words become your laws. And in the same way you can use words to change your perpetual thoughts. Hence the rise of affirmations. I'm going to be talking about the different forms of manifestations later, but I digress.

The techniques from my Manifestation Roadmap [which I'll be introducing later], mostly involve words. And when I talk about doing exercises, I actually want you to write those words down on a piece of paper. This is why journaling and writing things down on paper is much more powerful - because not only are you thinking those words, you have put pen to paper, you're taking concepts from the spiritual world and putting them into the physical world in your own words. That's why words are so, so powerful.

Okay, so we understand that thoughts are important. We understand that the only way to change our thoughts is through our words. And the only way that we can actually manifest something is through words, because those are powerful enough, and they will grow over a period of time until you eventually manifest what you want. When you understand the power of words, that is when manifestation goes through the roof, and you're able to manifest the kind of world that you want much more quickly.

Why are words so powerful? They are the self-fulfilling prophecies that I just mentioned. Think about the superstitions that we have, for example, the horseshoe or the rabbit's foot. Now, these are nothing more than weird superstitions, because those things have no power in themselves. But your spoken word holds power. When enough people say "This horseshoe is lucky, or the rabbit's foot is lucky" they start to believe it. It's the spoken word propagating the belief that it will bring you good luck. And that creates the expectancy in your subconscious mind that attracts those lucky coincidences.

That's how it works. That is why it's so important to be mindful of your words. Now, of course, it's going to be very difficult for you to be mindful of <u>all</u> your thoughts, especially when you're first starting out. Eventually you will get to grips with it. But if you use the tools that I give you, or any other mentors may give you, by systematically being conscious of your mind, by systematically thinking and retraining your subconscious mind, especially through energy clearings, you can become mindful of your thoughts, and you can actually train your mind to think positive thoughts for the majority of the time. There will be so many occasions when we fluctuate back and forth, but the majority of the time you can think positively. When you're first starting out, it's very difficult to get manage every single thought as we have, on average, seventy thousand thoughts in an hour, so it's very difficult to keep track of every single one. You can, however, become mindful of your words.

Remember, your words are more powerful than your thoughts. So if you start becoming mindful of your words, if you catch yourself saying something, for example "Oh I'm stressed, this never works for me, or money never turns out for me," when you catch yourself saying these words, in the back of your mind there could be ten or one hundred thoughts attached to that one particular sentence or word. The two words "I'm broke" have probably about ten thousand other thoughts attached to them.

Treat every single word that comes out your mouth with the utmost respect and be very careful about them. For example, if you're trying to manifest an additional five thousand dollars a month, or you're trying to gain another five clients for your business. or you're trying to build an online business or   a new offline business, but at the same time your words are actually saying the opposite. For example, you might tell yourself "The market is so rubbish right now. You know, the online space doesn't work", or "People are fraudulent," or "People just don't want to pay" or "People haven't got the money". If you're talking and saying words which are in opposition to what you want to manifest then it gives a clear indication of whether you're in alignment with your goal or not. It also tells you that you're not going to manifest, because the words you're saying are so powerful, and they are opposite to what you want. So not only do the words give you an indication of where your thoughts are, what you're projecting to the outside Universe, they are also creating your laws. If your words are, "This is hard", it becomes hard for you. If you think, "Oh, I can't attract high end clients", guess what? That becomes law for you. If you say, "I don't know how to manifest my ideal partner", guess what? That becomes a law for you, and you don't manifest that ideal partner.

Whatever you say, whatever words come out of your mouth, just be mindful that they then become your law. Now, this brings me to the next point, which is about jokes. Now, I'm very careful, I don't do self-deprecating jokes or jokes about other people. I don't make any comments that could cause harm or attract something negative, even as a joke. I don't call myself fat. I don't call myself this or that. When I talk to my daughter, I'm very careful how I speak to her, saying for example "You know, we need to exercise, become healthier." Not just for her mental state, but also because I don't want to start attracting those things to her or myself. How you speak to yourself, how you speak about your business and everything else; it's imperative that you are very careful about it, because the words you use will become your laws.

You can understand there are invisible forces which are always working. And you as a person, you're always pulling the strings for yourself, though you may not know it. You always have the Universe working with you, whether against you or for you; it always is. The vibratory power of your words is bringing things into existence or not, those thoughts start somewhere. Thoughts are something which everyone talks about, but I think the word is more powerful. Thoughts are things, but people forget. When you really begin to realise this, that's when affirmations work. That's why when you communicate with yourself through the mirror exercise, which I talk about later, that's why that works. Because when you speak it, you make the non-physical into the physical, and you bring it into the three dimensional world and actually make it happen. You bring this amazing energy into reality. And that's why words are so powerful. This is the first Law of Money - the power of words. Wherever you speak, whatever you say, it becomes your law. So whatever you're saying, (and this is not only for money, it also applies to your health) that's what will come to you, wanted or otherwise. If you believe yourself, if you keep saying "I'm just old, I've got old." Guess what? You'll be old! That's your law. Therefore, whatever words you use, whatever words you say, they become your laws. That's the first Law of Money, so be careful with the words you choose to describe yourself, to describe your business, to describe your lifestyle and other people. Stop talking about your past, stop talking about what happened. Stop talking about other things, if you need to vent it out, if you need to get it out, put it in a piece of paper and burn it. That's it.

Allow yourself some space and time when you can vent out and actually experience through all the negative things that you've experienced. Absolutely. Don't push it under the table, don't hold it in. But at the same time, don't be thinking, "I was a victim because this or that happened." Don't stay in the victim's energy. Because every time you repeat the words out loud, when you complain to people about your past experiences, you are bringing them back into your life - it's becoming your law. Are you understanding how powerful this is? So when you complain that "My mother went through this and my father went through that" you continue to be trapped. I say things and I say them with absolute neutrality, there's no emotion attached. I do this on purpose. I do it as a matter of fact, if I'm explaining my past or explaining how I manifested my mother's life. And I say it as a matter of fact, without any emotion attached, because I'm explaining something in the past. I'm not using it to complain, I'm not using it to fuel victim energy. Does this make sense?

When you complain about the ex-boyfriend, if you complain about your husband, the more you complain about something, this is why it happens again. Not just thinking about it, but speaking about it, when you speak something, you bring it into your world faster. It becomes your law and it's difficult to break. Because then it's right in front of you, it's showing its face, and then it's very difficult to change. This is why sometimes you need to ignore certain things, turn the other cheek so that it doesn't manifest rapidly. You can change it, and you can change things with your words as well.

Please understand this, as quickly as you've manifested the rubbish in your life, you can manifest the positive things. This is why when you say affirmations daily, when you speak about them with true positive emotions, those things manifest in life that much more powerfully and that much more quickly.

Let's recap the first Law of Money.

I've explained to you what energy is. I tried to explain it as succinctly as possible, what energy is and why thoughts are responsible for your reality, and how words are more powerful, that they actually create your laws, the laws that you live by in your life. Therefore, the only way that you can rectify this in any way, to change things in your life, is to change your words, and become very mindful, in terms of everything that comes out of your mouth, good and bad, and including the jokes you say about yourself.

In the next chapter we'll cover the second Law of Money and keep in mind, the way I describe things is always simple for a reason. The more complicated and convoluted something is, the less you'll understand. Thus I've made this Law very simple. When you go from here, be mindful of everything you say, not everything you think, because that's impossible, but everything you say. If you catch yourself saying something in the negative, say something positive in return, counter it with something positive. Moving forward, this is the way to apply it in your life. Be careful, be very mindful of every word that comes out of your mouth. If you say something which is not for your benefit, not something that you want to attract into your life, then as soon as you say it, acknowledge it [because remember, this is a habit that you need to break] and then say something positive in return.

If you want to say, 'I'm really worried about money today," then in turn you say, 'You know what, money flows to me effortlessly through multiple sources, it's increasing in quantity on a continuous basis, and it just happens all the time, you flow so easily to me, I'm in the direct flow of money." Do you see what I mean?

I will see you in the next chapter with the second Law of money.

CHAPTER 4

THE SECOND LAW OF MONEY – THE LAW OF NON-RESISTANCE

"Nothing can resist a person who is non-resistant... When you overcome negative with positive...hate with love... Evil with good. You've turn a loss to a win... You have become profound."

— Val Uchendu

Here we are with chapter four; we are now covering the Law of Non-Resistance. This is one of my favourite laws and this helps to explain a lot of things and a lot of how the metaphysical world works, how the Law of Attraction really works. And it's a principle that if you don't understand it fully, you will not be able to appreciate the Law of Attraction in its full glory.

We are covering the Law of Non-Resistance. This for me is the second Law. If you don't understand this Law, then all the others are negated to be honest with you. Therefore this is very important, the Law of Non-Resistance. I'm going to explain to you what I mean by the Law of Non-Resistance, and how you can apply it in everyday scenarios. Now, this is the perfect opportunity if you have questions about how to apply this in your particular area of life, ask me during one of our workshops, that'll be the ideal situation, you can ask me questions. Gull how do I apply this in my life?

So what exactly is the Law of Non-Resistance? Let me explain why Non-Resistance is so important. There's a saying that nothing on Earth can truly resist an absolutely non-resisting person. And according to the Chinese, the most powerful element on Earth is water. Why do I use water as an example? First of all, you can't get more non-resisting than water. Water doesn't bother you. If you're in its way, it'll find a way around you, on top of you, underneath you, it will find a way. Thus, it's the most non-resisting element, yet it's able to cut through mountains over a period of time. It can conquer anything, it's that powerful and yet it's very non-resistant. Water just flows. And that's what I use as symbolism for money. So the money just flows to you. If you're resisting, money will find an alternative, up, below, around and so forth. So for this reason, if you become non-resistant to it, you actually take on the principles of water, which are really powerful.

I'll give you an example: if you're standing there and someone's really angry and you're being non-resistant, you're not actually resisting this person, which means you're not smirking, which means you're not being sarcastic, you're not doing anything, you're just being in this really calm zone, like a monk [the image of that old eighties film, the Karate Kid comes to mind]. When the master is standing there and the teenagers are trying to do X, Y and Z, and then the teacher doesn't move. He's completely calm and poised. That's what you need to be in every situation. And if you are like that nobody can touch you. It's like when you're standing in that solid position, no one can dismantle you, no one can emotionally push you over.

Remember, you are responsible for your own emotional well-being, your own emotions, your own actions. You are not responsible for somebody else's actions, somebody else's emotions, somebody else's behaviour... you are solely responsible for yourself.

Regardless of how somebody is trying to provoke you, it doesn't matter. Regardless of what's going on around you, you become very centred, and you actually become very non-resistant; like water. So if you need to go in a particular direction, and there are obstacles in your way, you find a way around it, above it, below it, that's how it is – like water. This is why it's super important. So, the idea is for you to become like water, and to become non-resistant.

In the previous two chapters, it's abundantly clear to you that your subconscious mind is responsible for everything that shows up outside you, in the external reality. Whatever is going to show up is actually your subconscious mind's responsibility. The images in your subconscious mind which when you emotionalise, feeling those things on a continuous basis, and then sooner or later it manifests an external reality. This is what your subconscious mind does. If someone is sick, he or she has been picturing sickness. A poor person has been picturing poverty, and a wealthy person, a rich person is probably picturing wealth. Sometimes it seems unfair, but if you think about it, poverty breeds more poverty. Affluence breeds more affluence. People say it's unfair. Yes, it is. I'm not saying these things are fair. I'm saying these things simply are- full stop! So poverty breeds more poverty. Why? Because you see this lack and limitation. And then you think, "Okay, that's the norm, everything's lacking.". And therefore you think "That's pretty much it. This is how things are, this is the status quo." Therefore, when you think of how things are, guess where you end up? Because you're seeing poverty around you.

You're picturing poverty, so more poverty comes along. The reverse is also true, meaning when you are surrounded by affluence, if you're surrounded by wealth, you picture wealth and guess what comes? More wealth comes to you. This is where you've heard the old phrase that money attracts money. Money doesn't per se attract money. It's just when you see money, you believe there's an abundance of money and therefore you attract more.

This is a core element to understand before we go into the Non-Resistance part. Your subconscious mind is responsible for your external reality. So whatever you're picturing internally will show up for you externally sooner or later. This is a fact, this is how things are and there's no getting away from this. Now let's come on to the resistance part and why being Non-Resistant is so important.

In my Millionaire Mindset Mastermind program, I talk about reframing debt. I don't talk about getting rid of it, yes you need to put a plan in action, absolutely, the practical steps go later, but the mental aspect of the mindset and the energy around debt needs to shift first. You need to shift your mindset and energy around something before you can actually put action in place to rectify the matter, whether it is debt, your health, you want to become wealthy or whatever it is, but the first thing you need to deal with is a mindset and your energy around it. The example here is debt: if you're in debt and you agonise about credit card bills and so forth, guess what happens? You end up sinking further and further into your debt.

This happens so often, as people spiral downwards. Why? Because they're picturing a debt and even though you're resisting and trying to make money to repay the debt, you are constantly picturing debt and guess what happens - more debt shows up. It's NOT the fact that you are irresponsible with money - you could have a breakdown, your washing machine could break down, your car breaks down or part of your house goes into disrepair, you have to fix that, the manifestation shows up, it doesn't matter. The point is, the expense will show up, which means less money for you, or more debt for you. That is what happens. Now turn it the other way around. So the first thing is... whatever you're resisting, you stop. This is where faith comes in. Faith comes into whatever's coming up. Whoever is there, whatever situation is there for a reason - to give you a lesson, to help you grow in some way. This is where faith is important. If you think you're doing everything by yourself, you're not; you're a co-creator, not a creator. This is very important for you to understand. You are a co-creator, not a creator, per se. You need to trust that whatever's happening, whatever's showing up for you, that Divine Source Energy is helping you grow in the right direction, the best for you. It's important to acknowledge that you're in this situation in the first place. Sometimes you're easily put into the mud hole, because you need to learn how to get out, or to recognise the fact that this is a mud hole! Learning how to get out of this situation will give you the base point and the memory to get out of other situations, or prevent situations like that from occurring in the future. So this is where Divine Synergy comes in. That's another topic for another day, faith in Divine Synergy - it helps you to become very still, calm and composed.

We're using debt as an example. Say for example that you've got twenty thousand worth of debt and that really bugs you, or you've got two hundred thousand pound mortgages on your head, and you're very concerned about it. As long as you're resisting it, as long as you keep paying for it you will continue to give energy to it. More of the same, so more debt, more anxiety, more fears will show up.

The first thing to do is say to yourself "OK, this is what it is, I've got twenty thousand pounds debt. This is the debt that I have. Okay. What's the worst that could happen?" When you become emotionally detached from the outcome of what could go wrong, you become Non-Resistant to the situation. Does this make sense? When you get emotionally detached you are not attached to thinking such as, "Oh, if this goes wrong, that will happen." Ask yourself just what are your fears? If money doesn't show up on time, what will happen? Get detached from those fears. So if this situation doesn't change, or if this debt continues to grow, what is the worst that could happen? Face your fears of what could potentially happen if money doesn't show up.

This is when you need to write everything down. If the money doesn't show up, this will happen. Or if my debt goes up, that will happen. Or if I have debt, this will happen, so all of the fears and all of the emotions that come with a particular situation need to be written down. Then you need to counter it: you can use EFT (Emotional Freedom Technique), you can use your mind, energy clearings, whatever tools you use, but use a tool to clear it first so that you are detached from the outcome of whatever could possibly happen and go wrong. When you get detachment from the emotional response for whatever's going on, you become Non-Resistant to it. You're no longer concerned with the debt and therefore you don't pay attention to it. However, when you are not detached from it, even though you may think you are, you consciously and subconsciously keep thinking about and attract greater and greater debt.

Why? Because subconsciously you are aware of the fact that you have debt and your subconscious is giving energy to it. You have to work on reframing and getting detached from debt, because remember, as a society in general we abhor debt, don't we? If you have debt you are seen as a financial failure. Seriously, you are, and therefore you see yourself as a financial failure if you have debt.

Simply ignoring it, pushing it under the carpet, that's not going to cut it. You have to actually put effort and energy into it and actually get emotionally detached from whatever the outcome is that you're afraid of. And then when you are, that's when you become Non-Resistant. Back to The Karate Kid analogy: if this guy is coming to you and lashing out at you and they're screaming at you. I mean if someone's barging at you and about to hit you, move out the way. Don't attack. Do you see the difference here? Defending yourself is fine, but defending yourself by moving out of the way is better. Not actually resisting by punching them or anything, nothing like this. If someone's being verbally abusive to you, if you are calm, eventually they'll become quiet. If you give no response to them whatsoever. It's like you haven't even heard them. If you just look at them very calmly, how long would they continue to abuse you? Not very long, and then they'll feel stupid doing it. If you have somebody who's argumentative and they are trying to argue with you, if you don't respond, what would happen? Same thing with any situation you have become Non-Resistant to, you're not resisting the situation.

There's another thing: when you're resisting situations you are pushing against them.

For example, if I've got all these debts and I don't want my debt, I'm pushing against it. When you're pushing against debt, guess what you're doing? Giving it energy. Are you understanding how profound this is? I keep my teaching very simple to make sure that everybody understands it. However, if you can grasp it, it's so profound. And this is how lives turn around. When you stop resisting it, you stop giving energy to it, and when you stop giving energy to whatever it is, it will fall away. It has to by law. It can no longer sustain itself there, because there's no energy feeding it. The more you resist, even if you try doing the opposite to it, the more energy you're giving to the situation, the longer it will reside in your external world. This is a fact. Therefore you have to become Non-Resistant to it, you have to become a Buddha-like, Zen-like monk, whatever the situation is. Obviously, when you think of a Zen-like Monk, you think of someone screaming and shouting at them and they remain very calm. That is just a metaphor. But that applies in every area of your life.

This applies to me too, I'm still learning. I'm one of those parents; I do everything I do for my children and thus my world revolves around my children. When my children don't do something that I wanted them to do, I catch myself as a parent saying "Oh flipping heck, why can't you do it, why can't you understand?" And then I rant like a lunatic, like a lunatic mom. And then I realise, "Oh, what am I doing? I'm resisting the situation." So if I resist it, then my children will continue to behave in that way. Instead I become Non-Resistant to it. I don't ignore it. I just let it be. And now, eventually it's going to fall away, eventually it'll sort itself out. Is this making sense? I hope so because this is one of my favourite Laws.

Now, I've got a question. Somebody asked me this and I want to talk about it. As a parent, I think one of my friends said to me, "Well Gull, everything you're saying is fine, but how do you explain sickness in children?" And I just want to touch upon this. When you have children, it's like walking around with your heart on your sleeve.

Seriously, you just literally have a part of you outside of you all the time. So it's very difficult to remain calm and to remain Non-Resistant. But you have to, for this reason, because children are very sensitive to the repetitive thoughts of people around them. Between the ages of zero to seven, only the subconscious mind is fully awake, because the conscious mind hasn't been fully formed. Children absorb thoughts and ideas from people around them, especially the parents, especially the mother. Children can pick up on, and unconsciously attract illnesses and disaster to themselves, because they picked up thoughts and ideas from their mothers. Imagine if the mum is heard to say "Oh, if that happens, this will happen to my child".

I want to give an example about a very good friend of mine from college. And I use her as an example all the time, because there are four of us, four friends from college, where we did our A levels. We're all very brainy, and all of us did very well academically. Now, this one friend of mine became a teacher. She's a gorgeous girl, yet she has every fear under the sun. Her thoughts are, "I can't do this, because that will happen." I mean we'd go out and all of us would go to the same restaurant, and guess what, who gets food poisoning? She does. Because she has this fear of getting food poisoning. Nobody else will get it, she'll get the food poisoning. With her child as well, this will happen and that will happen. She brings all these disasters to her child all the time. And I'm flabbergasted and keep trying to tell her, but obviously you can only help someone as much as they want or are receptive to. I'm unable to help her, but I've seen how she attracts energy. She's not all that bad when it comes to children. But there are other parents who do bring a lot of illnesses to their children through themselves. I want to highlight this. As a parent, you need to be Non-Resistant and know that your children are fine: the more you try to control situations, the more they'll go out of control. This is the idea behind the Law of Non-Resistance. Don't try to control; water doesn't try to control anything, honestly, water does nothing, it just flows. That's the kind of energy that you need to hold within your own physical self. If you just flow, you don't resist, you have a direction which you're going in, because water always has a direction in which it is going - it always has an end goal in mind. Yet, it's always flowing. It's never resisting. It's never concerned with the obstacles in the way because it knows it will find a way around it, above it or below it. That's the kind of Zen-like mentality that you need to adopt. You know that whatever resistance shows up, you'll find a way above it, below it, around it or through it. That is the idea behind it. Does that make sense?

A person who's actually centred and has established the right thinking, a person who sends only goodwill to fellow men and women, and who is without fear cannot be touched or influenced by the negative thoughts of others. You need to see this, this is quite important for you to understand. I have been in business now for about three and a half years. I had a mentor who completely out of the blue, thrashed me for no reason. I had no idea why she behaved that way. That was an example where I showed Non-Resistance. Now, because of the way I showed Non-Resistance, after she behaved this way with me, my business took off. Can you see? She tried to say x, y, z about me. I blessed her, forgave her and did exactly what I'm telling you to do now. I was totally Non-Resistant to the situation. And because of that, instead of her damaging my career and my business, which I think was her intention, my business thrived, and I did exceptionally well. A year after this incident, I put my first international conference together in the Maldives. I went leaps and bounds from where I was when she attacked me. And this is purely by applying the principle of Non-Resistance, hence my love for this Law, the Law of Non-Resistance. You need to be in a place where you're so centred and calm that nothing can sway you, nothing can push you away, nothing can influence you negatively. If you know that everything's for your benefit, this comes back to the point of having faith. Every person we come in contact with, good and bad alike, is a golden link in the chain of our good. This is the phrase that I heard from one of my mentors. She said that every person you meet, every good and bad person, it doesn't matter what kind of encounter you have with them. Every single person is a golden link in the chain of your good. This is how you must see everything. You need to become Non-Resistant to situations. Is this clear? A question might come up, "How do I charge what I'm worth in my business?" That's not a question about Non-Resistance. What you can become Non-Resistant to is the idea of self-worth. If you are resisting charging what you want, or charging what you desire, see why you have a fear around it, and become Non-Resistant to that. A lot of the time if you're not charging what you're worth in your business, it's probably because you're resistant to the idea of what you want to charge. So if you want to charge five thousand for three months work, then somewhere along the way you discover you're resistant to it, ask yourself why? Figure that out.

How can you apply this principle of Non-Resistance to your life, with your spouse for example? You keep telling your spouse, "Take out the garbage," and she doesn't do it or you want them to fix something in the house, do some DIY work and they're not doing it. Now the more you nag and the more you resist that, the more you're resisting the situation, the more you should actually think "OK, fine, let it be, allow it to be, I'm not going argue, I'm going bless it." So you bless the situation. If, for example, the garbage hasn't been taken out and you're upset with your partner. Instead of being upset with your partner, you bless the partner. You say "I bless you [name]. May all your heart's desires come true, may you be happy in whatever you do." You bless the situation of whomever it is, you bless the person that you're resisting, does that make sense? And that blessing negates the resistance.

"Every person is a golden link in the chain of my good" is one of my favourite quotes. I love this. This is always in the back of my mind. If you can see it this way and truly apply it in your life, then you stop resisting people, you stop resisting situations. This includes your ex's, by the way. If you have ever had a narcissistic partner, and I've had a very narcissistic ex, I was able to forgive him for this reason, because I knew somewhere along the line, he helped me to learn and develop, where I wouldn't be doing what I'm doing if it wasn't for him. I wouldn't be prospering in my career if it wasn't for him, because if it wasn't for him, and I didn't go through the trauma and the pain that I went through, I wouldn't be who I am. And I wouldn't be able to apply the principles and teach the way I can. Because of the empathy I have, and the affection I have, and the understanding I have, I would not be a twenty-five year old earning six figures, I would not have the empathy of the single mum who was struggling to put food on the table. Are you with me?

It works with other people. When you bless people, for example, (if you're in a situation), you know that there's family gathering, and there's going to be conflicts or issues or whatever, bless that person, bless that situation and become water-like for it and just be very calm around it. This will help you to not get into that situation. The less you think about it, guess what, the less it'll show up for you, does that make sense? It's pure common sense to be honest. The less you think about a negative situation, the less likely it is for it to show up. The more you think about a negative situation, the more likely it will show up. This works for the positive as well. The more you think about a positive situation, the more likely the positive situation will show up, or things will start showing up which will reflect to you or show to you that thing can show up. Earlier today I was thinking, "OK, I'm doing this and this" and I was thinking about the money, "Where's the money going to come from?" Do you know what I found? A two pence coin on the floor. As soon as I thought "I need to get the money for this, I need to make sure that it's okay" and I was thinking, "How am I going to handle all the money for this month?" immediately I saw two pence on the floor. Now two pence in the UK is nothing for most people. But for me, it was symbolic. So I picked it up and I thought, "Thank you," and I blessed the situation and I moved on. So whatever expenses are coming up, whatever things are coming up, money will show up, money will turn up. Just get into the flow of it. Avoid resisting situations.

What about debt? Debt I would see not as a lesson necessarily. In my Millionaire Mindset Mastermind Program, I talk about changing the mindset around debt, as a way that these large institutions and these other big organisations see you as a credit worthy, honest and integral person, somebody who's worth taking a risk on. These large institutions have these really complex internal check systems and other things, to see you as an honest person with integrity and somebody who's creditworthy. That means that you are a trustworthy person, you're an integral person, so you change your image about it. Because debt has a lot of shame attached to it. Therefore, you must first change your idea around it for yourself, and then you bless it. Don't resist the debt. Bless your debt. Bless it. If you're twenty thousand in debt, bless that, you think "OK, you served a purpose, you helped me to do X Y and Z, I'm so thankful and grateful to you, the money showed up." Because remember, debts are money. We forget this - debt is still money in a different form, but it's still money. "Thank you for so much money showing up for me. Thank you so much debt, for showing up for me. You helped me to get through this" and just bless it. Bless the situation and stop resisting it. Know for a fact that the money you need will show up before you need it. Remind yourself out loud "I'm so happy the money always shows up before I need it" and accept that as reality for yourself. If you do, and when you do, you find money always shows up before you actually need it. It is always more than enough money before you need it. This is Divine Synergy telling you're taken care of. This goes back to the idea of faith - that you have to have faith in Divine Synergy that this is going to work for you in the most beautiful way possible.

One of my clients said "It has worked tremendously in my life recently with two relationships, and the transformation is undeniable, both are very easy". Wonderful, that's absolutely perfect. You need to be Non-Resistant to your relationships, especially your personal relationships, to your spouse, to your children, to your parents, to your in-laws, and even to neighbours and friends. Those are the ones who you resist the most - you get annoyed with them, you get in arguments with them, you get frustrated with them, and you can set them free. I have one example with one of my closest relations, which is my brother. With him, I always used to get upset about his situations, life choices and his current lifestyle. Now I'm being completely Non-Resistant to it, I bless him and allow him to be, and I know that's his life and his choices, he will change when he's ready or choose a different lifestyle when it suits him. So I'm Non-Resistant to it, I am going to be fully supportive and be ready to support him when he's ready. Recently he came to me for help. I told him "I can help you, I've got a successful online business, I'll set it up for you, but I'm not going to do it for you. You will have to pay, take the minimum cost, which isn't much," and he was resistant to that. He said, "Oh, that's too much money for me to pay at the moment". One hundred dollars and he's refusing. So when someone is like that, they're not ready to move forward, so you just let them be. "Come back to me when you are ready - come back to me when one hundred dollars is not too much money for you." And if I keep resisting him, if I keep thinking about him, guess what I'm going to manifest in my life? Lack or limitation, and the things that are showing up in his life will start showing up in my life. Is this making sense to you? I hope it does. The Law of Non-Resistance is the least understood of all these Laws. I think this is the one which is the least understood, yet it's probably one of the most powerful Laws out there and it is adopted by the most powerful element, water. Water is the most powerful element, because of this Non-Resistant nature. It's Non-Resistance for a reason, because it knows it can conquer anything, it can conquer the largest mountains over time. This does require patience and it requires faith, but you can do it. We all can. If you don't want it in your life, and you're upset or angry with it, the more upset or angry with it you are, the more likely it will show up and continue to show up in your life. If you want to remove it from your life, take the emotional charge away from it. Take the emotional response away from it, and you debilitate it and it's no longer applicable in your life. Let me know if there is any way I can help you to apply the principles of Non-Resistance to your life. This applies in all areas: your money, your business, your relationships, your business relationships, your friends, your neighbours, your children's lives, your children's teachers, your teachers, the children's schools, any situation.

This is in alignment with the art of allowing. Allowing people to be who they are and maintain the joy regardless. It's very similar, the same thing. But I think I go beyond it. It's for the greater good. The reason why I think it's more powerful is because this is when you take a step back and think "OK, Divine Synergy is responsible for everything." Divine Source Energy has a great complex plan of which you are a tiny, miniscule part. Everything happens at the right time to the right people in the right order. So everything's going according to the Divine plan. It's okay. I'm good. I'm taken care of, I've been protected and taken care of by Divine Source Energy and everything in my life will show up in the right way at the right time. Does that make sense?

Should you forgive debt? If you want to, if you feel that you have this anger and frustration with it, then forgive it. Then forgive yourself for having the debt. If you want to forgive someone then you forgive yourself, for having the debt, and you know you can use whatever modality that works for you such as Ho'o Pono Pono or EFT or my energy clearings, any of the modalities would work. But forgive the debt and forgive yourself because you're the one who got into debt. It doesn't matter if it's because your ex-husband did whatever thing, if you are in debt, regardless of the circumstances, you attracted it to yourself. Therefore you are responsible for it. Take full responsibility for every aspect of your life. Stop the blaming game, because you are attracting your life - you are co-creating a life with Divine Source

Energy, whether consciously or subconsciously, this is why my role is to come and tell you, let's change your life one day at a time. Let's consciously do it. Let's change your life for the better. I just absolutely love Non-Resistance for these reasons, and I hope you get benefit from it. Until the next chapter, I'm going to love you and see you very shortly.

CHAPTER 5

THE THIRD LAW OF MONEY – THE LAW OF KARMA AND FORGIVENESS [PART ONE]

"The universal law of karma ... is that of action and reaction, cause and effect, sowing and reaping. In the course of natural righteousness, man, by his thoughts and actions, becomes the arbiter of his destiny".

— **Paramahansa Yogananda**

We have covered the first two Laws of Money. We are now working on the third Law of Money. Again this one is wonderful if you know how to use it, if you understand it, it's absolutely brilliant.

For those of you who are spiritually minded, working on the spiritual path and spiritually guided, then this will explain to you why anytime you've done something bad, or something wrong happens or you take a step out of alignment with yourself, why do they give you a big Whammy in the back? Why do you suffer the repercussions a lot quicker than most other people who don't? Or they feel like a cheat and a fraud or whatever, yet nothing catches them. Whereas you tell one lie and you get caught, right? So I'm going to explain why this works. This is really one of those important Laws. I say this is like electricity.

You know I use metaphors for everything. So the Law of Non-Resistance was equated to being like water. Today's Law is going to be equivalent to electricity. If you know how to use this Law, you can absolutely powerhouse yourself and move forward at exponential speed. But if you don't know about this Law, and you don't understand it, then it could really come and hit you quite hard. That is why this Law is super important.

What is the third Law of Money? The third Law, according to me, is the Law of Karma. There's a lot to this, so I have actually split this up into two parts. In truth it's the Law of Karma and Forgiveness, because otherwise this chapter would go too long. So I'm going to cover the Law of Forgiveness in the next chapter. That means this part is actually the first half of it and it's the Law of Karma. A really, really important law, and I'm going to explain to you what karma means and what I understand of it. I will also explain to you why people who have high consciousness, good people, seem to suffer from this more. I'll explain to you how your will works and how to use your world with the Law of Karma? Let's get started.

What is the Law of Karma and what does karma mean?

Well, we often hear the phrase "Karma is a bitch" but what does karma actually mean? 'Kerma,' or karma is a sense of good. It's from the old scriptural Indian language and Hindi, which is an Indian national language that actually incorporates a lot of Sanskrit words. Sanskrit is an old traditional language used in India, and it actually means "come back." That's it, that's all it means: "Come back."

The idea is whatever you send out, you receive back. You know this; this is actually in the New Testament, in the Old Testament, in the Quran, in all the religious books. They all have this idea of what you sow is what you reap. There's a phrase, "What you give is what is received," we all are familiar with these almost clichéd phrases, but these clichés are very real.

Let me explain this. If you are a high consciousness person, if you are somebody who is very self-aware in that you're actually awakened... you're not sleeping, you're not on the sleeping plane, you're not walking around blindfolded, you understand the Divine Source Energy. If you do good, you know you're supposed to be good to people and you're a good person generally. You don't lie, you don't cheat. You're consciously aware; you're a consciously awakened person. Now, if you're that kind of person, and everybody reading this book is that kind of a person, because those kinds of people are attracted to me, the kind of clients and people I speak to tend to be people who have high consciousness, they are good people who do want to attain prosperity for themselves, but not just for themselves, for their family and their friends and for people in the world at large. People who are consciously awakened, those are the kind of people who are coming into my tribe and talking to me because that's the kind of person I am, so I attract similar sorts of people. So I can guarantee you that every single person reading this book - if you ever lie, if you ever cheat, if you ever do anything incorrectly or go against your better judgment, you get slapped on the wrist by nature or Divine Source Energy straightaway.

Yes there are people out there who could defraud, cheat and whatever - we all know the stories. People who've done bad things, but they get away with it. Nothing bad happens to them or if it does, it takes a long time. Whereas you could do one tiny thing wrong... For example, I've actually been very humble, as in I'm not arrogant at all. But if at any point of time I've said anything of arrogance or was ever rude to anybody, even if it wasn't intentional, I would get slapped on the wrist by karma. One time I remember I went to a restaurant and I was talking. I'm always nice to everyone on purpose, because I treat the doorman and the restaurant owner equally. The same way I treat the doorman, and the waiter, and the restaurant owner, and the manager; all equally. I'll give them equal respect and dignity because they all deserve it, regardless of their job. Yet I remember I was on the phone, the waiter came and he said "Can I take it?" and because I was busy on the phone that I didn't acknowledge him, I just said, "Yes take it." It was very rude of me. Instantly I picked up that my behaviour towards this person was rude. Now this is going back four years ago. I remember it so vividly in my mind because literally the very next day I had a meeting with somebody, and the person was exceptionally rude to me. Now, if you're consciously awake, when something bad like that happens to you, instantly your memory of what you've done will be flashed across your conscious mind. It will absolutely flash across to you reminding you that, "Oh, I did that to that person." The very next day this lady was exceptionally rude to me, she really put me down. But instead of being angry and upset with her, at that very moment that memory of the night before with the waiter flashed across my memory. I realised I've done them wrong and instead of being rude and angry at this woman, I actually blessed and sent love and blessings to the waiter, thinking, "I apologise to you for behaving this way. It was not my intention and I'm so sorry. I apologise profusely to Divine Source Energy and please send Divine Energy to that waiter." So you find at any point in time you are rude or do anything that can be construed in your own mind that you are behaving badly, or not in alignment with your highest self, you will get a slap on the wrist. Why is that?

Let me tell you why - that is because Divine Source Energy is keeping you on track. Imagine two people walking down a path. One person is on track and if they deviate even slightly, it's like "come back". Divine Energy says "Come back here onto this path." The other person has deviated quite a lot from the path. Now they're going to head to different destinations and they have their own roadblocks on the way.

It's not your job to work out when or how that person will be brought back on track or how to overcome the obstacles. You just need to know that, if this is happening to you, know Divine Source Energy is keeping an eye on you and keeping you on track. If you stay in alignment with your higher self, which means being good to all people, make sure that you don't lie, don't cheat, you're true to yourself and true to others, that is Divine Source Energy's way of keeping you on track. This is very important.

This means the money and prosperity you attract to your life, in your finances, and the prosperity in your health, in your relationships, it's actually good for you. It's going to help you, the relationships that come to you will give you love and joy, the friendships you'll have will give you ease and enjoyment. The health you have in the body you have will be healthy and vibrant. Does that make sense? It is really important to understand this though, when you're kept on track by

Divine Source Energy, this is why people who are consciously awake, people who are good people will actually suffer or get punished. We get punished a lot quicker than somebody who isn't consciously awake. Now, that's one reason.

The second reason is that with knowledge comes responsibility. Divine Source Energy is giving you knowledge for a reason. When you have knowledge about certain things, you have the responsibility of making sure that you adhere to it. This is really important as well. There's an old saying that says "ignorance is bliss". Well, I don't think ignorance is bliss. I think ignorance makes you feel as if God blindfolded you and you negate the gifts. When you do have knowledge it empowers you. It broadens your horizons. But at the same time, it gives you the responsibility of making sure that you look after your actions carefully, because of the karma that is going to come back. You are going to get hit by Karma if you're awake, and it will come back really quickly. Alternatively, if you're not consciously awake, it comes back eventually. It's like the boomerang theory - the longer it takes for the boomerang to come back, the harder the hit. Some people fall from grace; my ex is one of them, he's prospering even though he does whatever, I bless him, I don't want him to get a call, but at the same time I don't see any repercussions of his actions affecting him. But when they do, it's a lot more, it's with a lot greater force and for them to recover is a little bit harder. So keep that in mind as well.

The more one knows the more one is responsible for. This is one of the spiritual Laws. If you do not practice, if you are a spiritual person and you're aware of spiritual laws and you don't practice it, you will suffer greatly in consequence. I'm going to give you an example of this for myself. As you can see, I always use myself as an example because I'm a person who's growing and learning as I go. I am very honest and very authentic, I make mistakes. I have a great amount of knowledge and have a great amount of spiritual knowledge. I don't call myself a spiritual guru, but I can be seen as one and I have responsibility. Yet, if I don't follow those rules, if I don't follow the principles I teach, then I get slapped on the wrist really hard. The most recent example of this was in January last year. My business was booming, I exponentially grew and my business was absolutely thriving. Now in January, I formed a partnership with somebody else, yet I knew this new person wasn't energetically in line with me. I have talked about this before, I'm not going to say the name of the person, I believed that she was awesome.

I thought she was great. Her values weren't in line with mine. I thought those were just personal choices. Now, my intuition was screaming at me, absolutely screaming at me. But I did not listen, I thought, "No, I'm being judgmental." I kept going against my conscious beliefs. Now, when you go against your intuition, something like this, for me, it was a very big lesson. And I had to learn it the hard way. In the future I will come across more of these people and I will have this lesson to refer to, and I will come out better. Now because I didn't listen to my intuition at the time, I had a slap on the wrist. And I lost out both time-wise, and money-wise. Actually, it could have been reputation-wise as well because it could have really, really harmed my reputation. Everyone knows in the online space it is all about reputation. Because I am a person of integrity, I stick to my word. That person wasn't trustworthy, as I found out later. Because I didn't listen to my intuition, I got slapped very quickly, and I suffered as a consequence. My business halted even though I was on target for seven figures by the end of the year. That's no longer the case. That's fine. I'll hit seven figures next year. Fair enough. It's a delay of about six months. It's all right. It's okay. I'm cool with that. I learned lessons on the way.

Now I haven't spoken about the different karmas. I'm just talking about your personal karma, when you have spiritual knowledge, you're spiritually awake but you don't follow those rules. For example, for me, to be inspired by Divine action is very important. Listening to my intuition is very important. When I don't listen to my intuition, I get hit hard, more than the average Joe, because I now am spiritually awake. I've been given these gifts. I've been given this knowledge and when I don't utilise my knowledge, I get slapped on the wrist by Divine Source Energy. Karma said "Come back in alignment, come back onto the path." Because I have a role to play. When I fulfil this role of mine I'm going to be given a higher task - this is another conversation for another day but I just want you to understand why that is. When you become spiritually awake you are there to do a role, and then when you don't do it, you get slapped on the wrist. This is where karma comes in. This is karma for you. When you take an action which is not aligned with your higher good or your higher self, Divine Source Energy can bring you back on track by giving you the small lessons. That's all it does. This explains why if you're a good person, why you feel you've suffered repercussions, because a lot of people ask me, "Gull, I'm a good person but you know, I always get this and I get parking tickets, these things happen to me" or so-and-so are horrible. The question is "Why do bad things happen to good people?" The age-old thing I hear all the time. Why do bad things happen to good people? And my response is always this: this is where the law of karma comes in. Bad things happen to <u>all</u> people.

If you're attracting bad things, they will come to you. The only thing is, bad things happen to good people quicker because if they've done something wrong, and be honest with yourself, when something bad happens, you could equate it to something else. For example, if I've been rude to somebody, somebody will be rude to me. If I have not listened to my intuition, I will suffer the consequences a lot quicker than somebody else who wouldn't. Keep that in mind. Be honest with yourself, what is it that you're putting out? The more spiritually guided you are, the more honest, good person you are, the quicker you will actually suffer the consequences, which is a good thing by the way.

This is a good thing because one, it means you're on the right track with Divine Source Energy. Secondly, and more importantly, the longer it takes for that thing to come back to you, the harder it is going to hit you. To illustrate this, if somebody slaps me from an inch away, it's a small slap. But when it comes from far away and distant, it hits you a lot harder. Sometimes (a lot of times), you find people who, when karma finally catches up with them, it knocks them out for good and they're not able to get up again. This is why bad things are seen to happen to good people. It's not just happening to good people. It's because it happened a lot quicker that you notice it quicker.

Bad things happen to everybody because karma catches up with everybody. "Karma is a bitch" people say. I don't think Karma is. I think Karma is a beautiful Law. But people misunderstand it. People misconstrue it. People say "Oh, well, I see bad people getting away with it, but good people suffer from it." No, you see people having the repercussions a lot quicker because Divine Source Energy is keeping them aligned, keeping them on track. Whereas with the people who deviate on their path so much, Divine Source Energy gives them a bit of leeway. Karma gives them a bit of leeway. Eventually when karma catches up with them, it's a lot harder. The impacts are greater. Does that make sense?

I want you to understand this misconception - that, "Oh good people cannot have money, good people have bad things happen." No, not at all, good people can make money, good people can have good things happen to them but if you are consciously awake and you are aware of spiritual laws and you're not following the spiritual laws and you deviate from the spiritual laws you will be pulled back. This is a good thing again because Divine Source Energy is keeping an eye over you, keeping you on track and keeping you in line with yourself.

Now, how does Divine Source Energy see you? Divine Source Energy sees you as this perfect thing, you're a perfect energy, it sees you as perfect in every way, shape or form. Nothing ever happens to you without your interference. So there's an old saying, "nothing ever happens without the onlooker," and it's an ancient saying. This is the reason why - because before you can have failure, before you can have success, before you can have joy and before you can have sorrow, before everything you know swings into visibility, it has to go into imagination. This is where the Law of Karma really comes in. Whatever is happening to you is because of all the energy you are sending out. This is important for you to understand - if you can take one thing away from this chapter, then please understand this as it's very important. This is the personal responsibility aspect, and I keep going on about how personal responsibility comes into it. Whatever is showing up in your life, you are sending out the energy for it.

That is the Law of Karma. Whatever you are receiving in your life is because of you sending out the energy in the first place. You cannot be happy, you cannot be sad, you cannot be fat, you cannot be thin. You cannot be tall enough. You cannot be wealthy, or poor, without first seeing it. Now this could be a subconscious imagination or conscious imagination. You cannot change your life without accepting personal responsibility first, and the Law of Karma dictates whatever is happening in your life, both good and bad, is because of you. Therefore if you're sending out energy that is perfectly aligned with what you desire, the Divine Source Energy will receive it and will see you as perfect. Then it would give you whatever you want - perfect health, perfect happiness, perfect love, perfect money, until whatever you want is interfered with, the image is interfered with, with your thoughts, your actions.

Now, coming back to the basic idea which most people have - the idea of the Law of Karma, that whatever you do to others, will happen to you. If you're bad with other people, bad things will happen to you. That's absolutely true. Not only bad things, but bad thoughts as well. We have a saying in Urdu. I think you'll understand if I phrase the sentence in English.

It means when you dig a grave for someone else, you end up falling in it yourself. But why? For two reasons. First of all, your focus is on digging the grave, so you're attracting a grave into your life. Secondly, the energy you're sending out is for somebody to fall on the ground, or falling into a grave. Metaphorically speaking, it also means we're going to try and do something bad to someone. When you are thinking of doing something bad to someone, you're attracting it into your own life. That's what the Law of Karma means.

This is one of the things that my children know inside out, and they throw back at me all the time. You see, I'm a very patient person. I don't have any rage or anything like that at all. I'm a very calm person. Yes I'm a very passionate person, but a generally calm person. But in the car, I'm used to driving very fast. I've slowed down a lot because I'm a mommy driver now. But I do find that people who don't drive properly or if someone cuts me out, or when people misbehave on the road I'll say "What an idiot!" That's when one of my children, my daughter or my son will come and say, "Mommy, your brain is listening!" That's the way I've taught them, that whatever you say will happen to you because your subconscious mind is always listening, and will reiterate to you, from this psychological point of view. Energetically, it's the same thing. I'm sending out this negative thought for this person. So of course, negative thoughts are going to go out and I am a spiritually awake person, guess what's going to happen? It's going to come back to me very quickly. If I wasn't a good person, it would have come back to me eventually, but maybe at a slower rate.

The Law of Karma says that whatever you send out, good and bad, is going to come back to you. This is where the Law of Forgiveness is really important. There's an important element which we'll cover in the next chapter, you have to read that too because this law is actually covered in two parts, as I said at the beginning. Honestly, the Law of Forgiveness is an integral part of the Law of Karma. But for now this is important: whatever you're sending out, you're going to get back. It doesn't matter if you DON'T act on thoughts like, "I'm going to go and kill him!" The fact that you've said that, the fact that you thought that is bad enough whether you take action on that or not is something separate. It's quite important for you to understand that your thoughts are really powerful and when you are thinking negative thoughts about somebody, even if you think you're a good person, they are still going to come back. If you're one of those people who are generally considered to be a good person in that you are kind, considerate, and you're generally aligned with your higher self, you're doing good deeds for people... if you have bad thoughts, trust me, bad things will happen to you a lot faster. It's not because Divine Source Energy dislikes you or hates you, it's because Divine Source Energy loves you. It wants you to stay on track. The more you deviate from the path the harder it will be for you to come back to it. So the best thing to do is - when you deviate from the path of your higher self - Divine Source Energy will find a way to bring you back on track, sometimes with brutal force. That is a third Law. This is very important and I want you to understand this fully.

What about freedom? What is freedom? The freedom of all, and happy conditions, comes through knowledge and spiritual law. This is why you have additional responsibility. If you are spiritually awake, you know you can have financial freedom, you can get freedom from your health problems, from your personal problems, from relationship problems, you get freedom from every thought or unhappy situation in this life, with the knowledge of spiritual laws. Yet with the knowledge of spiritual laws comes the responsibility that comes with them. The responsibility of knowing the spiritual laws, so you are obedient to them. Being obedient is being very careful of your thoughts for other people. This is so important.

Now this is where I mentioned the fact that it's like electricity, now you know the law. The Law of Karma is as powerful as electricity. If you don't know how to handle electricity, you can kill yourself. You can literally kill yourself, it is that powerful, but if you know how to manipulate and use energy - if you know how to obey the laws of electricity, then you know how to have a refrigerator that works. My fridge works with electricity normally, my laptop and everything else. We can have amazing things once we know the laws of electricity. It's the same thing with the Law of Karma. If you don't know how to deal with it, it's not just about having positive thoughts in general, it's about sending positive thoughts towards people.

Now, if you've done my Boot Camp and my other programmes you know that I frequently talk about forgiveness. I want to go into a whole chapter on that later. But that's the second part of the Law of Karma, because you cannot send negative energy towards other people who've been bad to you. This is imperative; you need to understand this point. If someone's rude to you, if someone's angry at someone, if someone did something bad to you, the Law of Karma dictates you have to forgive them. Don't seek revenge. There's another old saying "An eye for an eye and blood for blood". I don't agree with it, and this is the reason why - because when you start thinking negative thoughts about somebody, you're sending negative energy out. The Law of Karma dictates that everything you send out energetically, YOU WILL RECEIVE back.

Now understand this, it doesn't matter how right you feel, or how much your ego tells you you're justified because the individual was rude and obnoxious, if you feel negative emotions, that's what you are sending out to the world. I'm going to give you an example. Recently, I was in a cafe and it was a friendly meeting with a group of people. We were talking about money and there's a gentleman there. Lo and behold, he was interested in me. I was unaware because I was talking about money. I wasn't really paying attention to things around me because I was engrossed in the conversation. Now this gentleman actually gave me a very nice compliment, and I was a bit taken aback. He said I was very interesting to listen to and talk to and I was very pretty etc. Then he asked me out. Now he expected me to say yes. However, I accepted the compliment by thanking him, but said I was not interested. I said it as nicely and politely as I could. That's when he became really rude to me. At every comment I made he made an obnoxious comment in return. I could have been rude back to this person, I could have been horrible to this person. If it was me from ten years ago, I would have been, but now I know better. So I didn't. I blessed him and I kept blessing him. I could have been really angry. Instead, I took the compliment and I remember him with a smile because he gave me a very nice compliment. I know all the snarky comments afterwards were just from his ego. Therefore I have no ill feelings toward him whatsoever and I didn't send him any ill will either. My ego could have felt justified; "Gull, he was so rude, Gull, he could embarrass you, he was trying to belittle you, Gull he was trying to undermine you." I could have felt those things, but I didn't. It was his male ego hurting and his ego was coming back at me. I put it in context and that's because I'm spiritually aware. Energetically I'm very aware - I can feel when somebody is attacking me energetically so I can protect myself. I simply cut chords with him and I protected myself and again, I did not send him negative thoughts. I accepted the compliment and understood his intentions and those of his lower self i.e., his ego. Therefore I chose to bless him and send him positive energy instead.

It took literally a few hours and he was gone from my life. I don't know if he remembers me, and I don't really care. However, that's the memory that I have, and I've chosen to keep the compliment as the presiding memory. All of his other behaviour I've just blessed him and let it go. There's no need for me to be angry at this person. When I'm angry at him, when I'm angry at somebody who's been bad to me, guess what I'm doing? I'm sending out karmic energy against myself because remember, the karma will just come back to me. When you forgive someone, you are not forgiving their actions. You're forgiving any idea in you to have revenge, any idea in your energy field to feel bad about the situation. You are letting yourself off the hook so that karmic energy won't come and bite your behind. If you do anything bad to any person – it doesn't matter how justified you think you are - it will come back to haunt you, you will get repercussions. You always have repercussions. That's why there is a saying that "Crime never pays." This is why it doesn't matter how justified you are.

Lessons from the wise!

What do all gurus have? What do all spiritual leaders talk about? I think somebody said to me that I am the one who talks about forgiveness the most in my practice. If you come and work in any of my programs or you any of my teachings... forgiveness is the first thing that I teach. It's one of the first things I advocate and I give you practical tools to forgive everyone from your past and present irrespective of whatever bad things that occurred in your life, do not reciprocate them. Now, I'm assuming you're not inclined to reciprocate the bad behaviour anyway. I find that anyone who is attracted to my teachings, and that includes anybody who's reading this book are generally people with high moral compass, and are compassionate and forgiving souls. I attract people who are not inclined towards revenge and are generous in nature.

At times you'll catch yourself thinking negatively about people. Please, please pay attention to this because nobody's talking about this and I want you to understand what's happening here. At times you'll be doing your work, you'll be at your laptop or you're cooking something and instantly a person comes into your mind. Instantly you have negative thoughts about that person. What does that mean? That means that the same person is thinking negatively about you and they've chorded it into you negatively.

Now what can you do?

Generally what you'll do is start thinking negatively about them, because your energy is reciprocating them. That's your natural reaction. What do I do? For example, my sister in law, my brother's wife, she'll come into my mind and I've got these negative thoughts about her. I'd ask myself "Why am I thinking negatively? Why am I thinking all these things about her? What is it?" Then I will see what's going on. And then what I'll do is - I know for a fact that she's sending me negative energies, she's sending me negative, energetic daggers. I'm protected. I know my shield is protecting me so now she can't really damage me in any way. I'll cut cords with her and then I'll set about sending her blessings and love, and forgive her for those actions. See the difference? So when she's sending me all these negative things, I start sending out blessings and love and send her good thoughts instead. And that is Karma. I hope you enjoyed this chapter. Now let's talk about forgiveness, which is the second element of the Third Law of Money, in the next one.

CHAPTER 6

THE THIRD LAW OF MONEY – THE LAW OF KARMA AND FORGIVENESS [PART TWO]

"To forgive is to set a prisoner free and discover that the prisoner was you."

— Lewis B. Smedes

We are on chapter six; talking about the third Law of Money. This is part two, because we have already covered the first part in chapter five – it's quite important and is divided into two parts: The Law of Karma, and the Law of Forgiveness, which when combined together make up the third Law of Money. They go hand in hand, and I do really believe in forgiveness. Therefore I decided to split the two up. I think the Law of Forgiveness deserves its own chapter by itself, because it's such a super powerful law that you need to understand.

We have a lot of people who don't understand the concepts of forgiveness truly and have misconceived ideas about the Law of Forgiveness. It's imperative that you understand it. For me as a money mindset expert, as somebody who deals with money and talks about money all the time, the Law of Forgiveness is paramount. I think the Law of Forgiveness supersedes everything, absolutely everything else for me. If you come and work with me, either in my Millionaire Foundations, or in my Mastermind, or even in a one to one, you will notice that I go heavily into forgiveness, in all areas of your life... for yourself and others.

Forgiveness, for me, plays a major part in my life. It is important, and I do say this time and time again that forgiveness is the path to prosperity. It really helps to focus on gratitude. Now a lot of people focus on gratitude, doing affirmations and the like. If you come and work with me, my focus is on forgiveness. I'm going to explain to you why.

Now in the last chapter we covered the Law of Karma. The idea of eye for an eye is a false notion in most of the religions that I see, and probably the one thing that I disagree with. I'm not a religious scholar, so I cannot say if it's right or wrong, everyone's is entitled to their own beliefs. But I would say that the only thing that I have an issue with when it comes to organised religion, is this notion of an eye for an eye, or a life for a life and so forth. I can talk about my own religion because I'm Muslim. I can say without offending anybody, in Islam there is an eye for an eye, but forgiveness is better. Whether you agree with that or don't agree with that, it's entirely up to you. I'm going to move forward and say that the reason why forgiveness is so important is because the "Eye for an eye" mentality, perpetuating this idea of revenge gets you nowhere other than a cycle of repetition and violence.

My thinking is that if somebody has actually done you wrong, or someone's being mean to you or cruel to you, you have to stop the energy there and then and you have to focus on your karma. You have to work on your energy, not theirs. This is the first part of it. The second part comes in, because you can't let go of that until you forgive this person. Thus forgiveness is of paramount importance. In this chapter we're going to talk about the Law of Forgiveness, and how and why it works.

First of all, let me start by saying that when you forgive someone, you're not condoning their actions. This point is important for you to understand. When you forgive somebody who has been mean to you, cruel to you, horrible to you, or has done this world a great disservice, you are not actually condoning their actions, you're not saying what they've done is correct. It's quite the contrary; what you're doing is cutting off their energetic connection to you, your ideas and your energy. That's what you're doing. You're saying, "OK what you've done is this, and I think it's really horrible. But I forgive you for it, because I'm going to allow your soul to deal with it." Everybody has their own journey. Everybody has their own soul contracts. I'm not going to go too much into soul contracts right now, that's another conversation for another time. For now, know that everybody has their own soul contracts, they have to do whatever they do, and they do it individually for themselves or to themselves separately. That's for them to do. What you need to focus on is your own soul contract. Focus on your thoughts, your ideas and your actions. There will be occasions when an individual misbehaves with you or upsets you through their actions or inactions. You may feel temporarily annoyed or upset with them. This is normal. I am not suggesting that you have to love all people all the time. You may even have revengeful and angry thoughts, that's fine too. However, what I ask of you is to very quickly remove such thoughts from yourself and it goes without saying, not to act on such foolish thoughts.

I'm here to tell you, you need to be accountable for your thoughts, not just your actions. This is a really important concept to understand. I really want you to take full responsibility for your thoughts, as well as your actions. This notion in society that we grew up with, that as long as you don't take action that's okay, so you can carry on thinking bad about people. As long as you don't actually go out and do those bad things, you're okay.

No, you're not.

You need to disconnect and dissociate from all negative thoughts about anyone for anything, regardless how much of your ego is justified in thinking those bad things. The problem is, your ego comes into play. Let me give you my example because I'm very transparent about this. Everyone knows that my ex-husband was abusive and cheated on me. Then he pulled the financial card, because I was going to divorce him. Even though my children and I were financially dependent on him, he took all of that away. By the way, to this day, he doesn't pay me anything, not even child maintenance. His excuse is he doesn't have any money, but that's another conversation for another time.

Now, the thing is I caught him in the act literally – I walked in on him and his girlfriend, so I had to forgive him... and I did it very, very quickly. Within the space of a few months. It didn't take that long to do it. I forgave him. *I didn't forgive him for his sake, I forgave him for mine.*

You forgive people for your own sake, not theirs. His actions were wrong, yes they were. What he did was wrong. He behaved badly with me. Yes, he did. But this Law meant that while I was stuck in that anger, that energy of anger, hatred and annoyance and victim energy, what does that attract to you? Like attracts like. The Law of Attraction by definition will keep bringing back to you the same energy. This is vital for you to understand.

If you want to seek revenge and you're angry, what will be brought back is the same energy. Now, when you forgive somebody, you disconnect from that energy. You say "What you did was wrong, but I'm going to bless you and leave you and move on." People talk about forgiving and forgetting. I go one step further. When I was forgiving my ex-husband, I went to bless him and even now to this day, when I think of my ex I bless him. Apparently he doesn't have a car or doesn't have much money. Every time he comes on the weekends, he comes in a really broken-down car. Yet yesterday, by pure chance, he had to come and collect my child because I had meetings and I wasn't able to get back in time. He was driving around in a Range Rover. How ironic! When I saw him yesterday in his car, I knew that was his real car. The one he brings on Sundays is just to show me that he doesn't have money. I blessed him and his car. In my head, I said "I wish you all the success." I blessed him.

Now, this is very important. Why did I do that? Because when I saw the car, I felt a little bit of resentment come up thinking, "Well, if he has the money to buy this car, how can he say he doesn't have money to support me for bringing up his children?" I'm human, it's logical. This thought would come up in anyone's mind. "I work so hard, I'm struggling between all my businesses setting all of this up and if he just supported me financially a bit more, it would give me a bit more ease in terms of bringing up the children contribution-wise, time-wise or money-wise. I'm normal, it's a normal human reaction to have that thought. My instinct was "Oh, okay", because I recognised,

"Oh, I don't want any resentment to come through," so what did I do? The way to counteract it, was that I blessed him. I forgive him beforehand, and I forgive him again for not contributing, doing what he should be responsible for, taking responsibility for his children, I blessed him and I blessed his car, and I wished him well.

Now when I'm sending out that energy of wishing him well and blessing him, what kind of energy am I getting back? What energy could I <u>possibly</u> get back? What could the Universe pick up and get back to me? Blessings and prosperity of course. I'm staying in the energy of blessings and prosperity and sending it out to the Universe - even to somebody who I shouldn't really like that much and should be annoyed at. I don't do that, even with my ego screaming at me, "Gull, what the heck are you doing? You're justified in being angry because he's been x, y and z." But the normal intelligent money expert inside me said, "Gull, no, he is just one channel." Even if he did pick up the financial responsibility for his children, he would become a channel of money for me, not the source. If he was giving me child maintenance, and he was paying financially for the children, he would be a channel from which I receive money, also not the source. If my source of supply is Divine Source Energy, then I can ask Divine Source Energy to give me my supply through another channel.

Therefore there's no resentment towards him. At the end of the day, my source of prosperity is coming from Divine Source Energy. It's not coming from a person or a job or a means. This is essential for you to understand. That knowledge will allow you to disconnect from any anger, annoyance or frustration that was between me and him.

How do you disconnect from something? Think about - if someone has crossed you, if someone has said for example, mean things about you, disconnect from the situation. "This person has said these mean things about me". Okay, first of all, if somebody thinks about you, it's none of your business anyway - keep that in mind. *You mind your own business, what somebody thinks of you is none of your business.* The reason being, if they are talking negatively about you, they're intermingling with that negative energy. As long as you don't connect with that energy, you are not part of it. They can say whatever they want about you, it will not be a reflection of who you are. Your character is the reflection of who you are, not what someone says it is.

Secondly, as I covered in the last chapter on Karma, if you automatically start thinking negative thoughts about someone it means they are bad mouthing you – they most probably are sending negative energy towards you, or they're having negative feelings towards you. Simply disconnect with them. The best way to disconnect from any negative energies is to send them blessings. If you know someone has said something bad about you, guess what you do? It's the thing that you hear from all religious texts: turn the other cheek. This is what turning the other cheek means - not actually physically turning the other cheek but actually sending them blessings. What will that do? It will stop the negative actions, the negative energies coming towards you, plus you're now in a positive energy. So guess what you're going to attract?

This one person may be saying negative things about you. If you disconnect by sending blessings back, now you're in the energy of blessings and love and prosperity. Guess what the Universe will pick up? Love, blessings and prosperity. Guess what you'll find? You'll have ten other people saying good things about you. Can you see how powerful this is?

Remember: when you forgive someone, you're forgiving someone for your own good, not for their good. You're forgiving for your own blessings, not their blessings. When you send blessings to somebody who's been mean, rude and cruel to you, what you're doing is you're sending blessings to yourself indirectly because you're sending it to the Universe. "I love the world. I love this place. I love you." Guess what the Universe picks up? Love, prosperity, joy and abundance. The Universe has to reflect back what's in your heart. What do you get back from the Universe? Love, blessings, abundance. One person says mean things to you, ten people show up with good, positive and uplifting things about you.

My ex is but one channel, as an example (a channel to bring in money). I sent him blessings that way. And the very next day we've got money coming in from my company. I've got my other businesses showing up. I've got clients showing up. My supply is over there - it's coming from a different channel, but it's still coming from Divine Source Energy. Why? Because I'm sending a blessing. I'm sending positivity and you can't do that without forgiving. Saying superficially "Oh, I forgive people," is not enough.

You have to bless them. You can justify to yourself being rude, being horrible, being rude back or cruel back or you take revenge. Even when you're justified with those actions, you should not take those actions and you should apply the Law of Forgiveness instead. That's the idea behind this. The Law of Forgiveness is the second element of that third Law; they go hand in hand. You employ the Law of Forgiveness, not to condone other people's actions, you do it to actually relieve yourself and disconnect from the negative energy that is surrounding a situation, or a person. This applies in every area.

Going back to the example of my ex; he is financially responsible for the children, but he's not paying, he's actually going out of his way to prove he cannot afford as he is not making much money. He brings in a really shoddy horrible car on a Sunday. The point being, instead of being upset and angry with him, because he has a really expensive car, I forgive instead. I know for fact that he's going out with young girls, and he's spending the money that he should be spending on his children on these girls and other things. I admit I was a little bit annoyed. Part of me was a bit annoyed because I'm spending all this time on all the businesses just to make sure that his children are well taken care of financially or otherwise. A small thought did come to mind that I was annoyed and there was a bit of resentment. But it quickly got crushed. I quickly got rid of him, by sending him blessings, and recognising a very, very important part. Now I'm repeating myself because this is an important point for you to understand.

My ex was just a channel for my supply. So if he pays now, according to the court order, he's supposed to pay me over a thousand pounds a month in child maintenance. He doesn't pay me a penny of that. Now if he did, he'd be one supply. Whereas the <u>source</u> of my supply, the source of my abundance is Divine Source Energy. So instead of him being a channel, that channel that dried up for me, I have other channels opening up to me and I have multiple businesses and I'm doing very well. You need to recognise the fact that your and my source of abundance is *always* Divine Source Energy. My ex was just a supply, it was just a channel and that has now dried up. But I've got others. Okay, that's the first development.

Secondly, and this is really importantly, if I stayed in that energy of resentment, if I stayed in the energy of anger, if I stayed in the energy of frustration, guess what I would be sending out to the Universe? Anger, frustration, sadness, and all of that. All of those negative energies disappear, by staying in the energy of forgiveness, and staying in the energy of blessing and prosperity. I had a little bit of resentment when I saw his car, I just thought, "Oh, it would be so much nicer if he took responsibility for his kids." That's it. That's all I had to say. I recognised "Oh my goodness, resentment coming up", so I sat down, and I sent him blessings to his relationships, and I blessed his car. Can you see how much I blessed him?

Now whether those blessings reach him or not, isn't my business - that's between him and Divine Source Energy, it's between him and the karma in his actions. What he does in his own life, it's his actions and his things. It's got nothing to do with me. I'm only responsible for my actions and my energy, so I can send blessings to every single person on the planet, whether or not those people receive the blessing is between them and their Divine Source Energy - that is their business. It's none of my business.

I can only look after _my_ energy, I can only look after _my_ thoughts and _my_ ideas and make sure that I remain in the energy of prosperity, forgiveness, joy and blessings. When the Universe and Divine Source Energy pick up my energy, what can they reflect back to me? The energy I'm sending out which is the energy of blessings and prosperity and so forth. This is why, when it comes to the Law of Forgiveness, you will be in a battle with your ego, your lower self against your higher self. I'm not going to go into too much detail about your higher and lower self but understand that, your ego is your lower self. Your ego will say, you're justified since all of these things happened, or for example if someone's rude to you, you're justified - he was rude to you, you should be rude back, or she was rude to you, you should be rude back. Or somebody is talking behind your back, saying X-Y-Z. You feel justified, so your ego feels justified in behaving in a certain way. This is why this Law is so important. It says "Hang on a minute. Yes, I am right. I am right to think that way. I'm right, I'm correct and right in reflecting that back, but do I want to be right or do I want to be happy? Do I want to be right, or do I want to be rich? I have this famous saying, *"You can be right or you can be rich, choose to be rich"*. I choose to be happy. So yes if someone said these bad things to me, I'm going to choose. Remember, you don't know what their ego is doing, you don't know what their situation is, you don't know what contexts they are living in. Therefore, choose to give that person the benefit of the doubt. They're living according to what they know. Who knows what they know? I'm choosing to disconnect with the negativity, I'm choosing to disconnect with their lower self, and I'm choosing to bless them.

If you recognise all of a sudden, the thought of someone, and then all your negative thoughts have come back to someone, recognise the fact that person may or may not be saying bad things about you or feeling negative things about you. If they are sending negative energy I'm not going to receive it. The way to disconnect and not to receive that energy is to send blessings back. Just as in Star Trek they'd say "Shields up," the Law of Forgiveness becomes a shield for you. They're sending through the ether of the Universe all this negative energy towards you; you put the shield of forgiveness up, and send them blessings back.

Now they may continue to still have negative feelings here. Two things can happen. One, they could actually start having softer feelings and actually become positive towards you. I have seen this happen; I have seen this happen so many times, when somebody has been thinking negative thoughts about you. And when you send them blessings back, they stop feeling negative towards you. Secondly what will happen is their negative thoughts and their negative energy will stop reaching you – they will stop impacting you, and stop bringing your energy down. This is super powerful. The Law of Forgiveness can act as a shield for you to deflect all this negative energy and make you prosperous. When you're in that energy of forgiveness - of, "I wish you well, you know whatever has happened, it's okay, I forgive you for everything, I bless you and I love your higher self" that is when you know you are attracting nothing but joy, happiness and prosperity back.

The Power of Love

"Love is power, the purest power and the greatest power: Love is God. Nothing can be higher than that. But this power is not a desire to enslave others, this power is not a destructive force. This power is the very source of creation. This power is creativity. And this power will transform you totally into a new being. It has no concern with anybody. Its whole concern is to bring your seeds to their ultimate flowering."

— Rajneesh

You've probably heard of Ho'o Pono Pono technique. You can say these four short sentences. *I'm sorry, please forgive me, thank you, and I love you. You can use these four sentences to forgive absolutely anyone for anything.* I use it in my practice and it's used by my clients in my Mastermind. Or you can just say, *it's okay, I forgive you, and I love you.* You're going into the energy of forgiveness and the energy of love. The energy of love is super powerful. Now, you might ask me the question, "Gull, how can I love someone who's been mean to me, how can I love someone who's so cruel to me?" I want you to understand who you are. You're a spiritual being in a physical body having a physical experience. That's so important, I'm going to repeat it: you're a spiritual being in a physical body having a physical experience. It could be your uncle, your aunt, your neighbour, your friend, your colleague, your boss, your ex-husband, your child, whoever. That individual is also a spiritual being in a physical body having a physical experience. They may not be awakened yet. They may still be sleeping, and they may not be spiritually awake. They may be working with the lower self and in the energy of anger and frustration. But in the end, we're all connected to Divine Source Energy. That means we are all one; the collective Consciousness is one. This maybe is a bit too much woo woo for this chapter, but I'm just going to give you the background in terms of why I'm able to forgive people so quickly.

If you were to look at your hand, imagine the individual fingers are people. Most people are walking around and all they can see is the top part of the fingers. They can't see the bottom half, and they can't see the connection. People who are spiritually awakened like myself, we see the connection; we can see that the fingers are attached to the palm. All of the fingers are all part of the same collective Consciousness, therefore the little pinkie cannot hate the index finger without harming itself, because we're all part of the same thing. That's how you understand that we're all part of the same thing. Therefore, you can love, as the pinkie loves itself, it has to love the index finger also because it's part of the same thing, it's part of the same hand, it's part of the same collective Consciousness. This is super powerful for you to understand - this is where the love comes in.

Therefore, if someone upsets you, you can say in your heart and mind , "You know what, I forgive you for what you did. I bless you, I love you." And really feel the love from your heart for them, at least their higher self, the spiritual side of them. If you can remember that whenever a negative point comes up, say, "I forgive you. And I love you and I bless you" you will find forgiving people becomes a habit after some time and very few things trigger you or keep you in the energy of anger and disappointment and frustration. Now there will be occasions when you might find saying "I love you" a bit too difficult, because someone has been really cruel or been really mean to you. It's very difficult to get to the energy of love that quickly. Then say this, "I forgive you and I bless you." Come from that energy and very, very quickly you find you change, your energy will shift, your anger will shift, and the negative thoughts and energies you're having towards a person will shift. Then you can start saying the words, *I love you*. Then you get into the energy of love, which will absolutely change your reality. Because what are you predominantly sending out? Predominantly you'll be sending out the energy of love, blessings and forgiveness out into the Universe.

Guess what's going to come back to you? Love, prosperity and forgiveness from the Universe. The Universe will actually take care of you and give you what you want. This is why the Law of Forgiveness goes hand in hand with the Law of Karma. As a combination they make up the third Law of Money. When you have negative energy from people or incidents, unless you forgive them, you're trapped in that energy. You will continue to attract the same sort of energy towards you and your finances. Now, a lot of people think, "Gull, how is me being angry at my neighbour going to reflect on my finances?" I'll tell you why. The reason is, regardless of the reason why you're angry at someone, if you're angry, if you're upset or if you're frustrated, guess what kind of energy you're sending out to the Universe? Regardless of the reason and regardless of how justified your reason is, the Universe doesn't care how justified you are - the fact is that YOU are sending out the wrong energetic vibration.

The important question to ask oneself is what energy am I sending out? You are like the satellite; you're sending out information or receiving information. Regardless of how justified you are to be tuned into the wrong, the point is you will only receive what's on that channel. If that channel has emotions of anger, frustration and sadness, then the Universe can only send back to you the same frequency that you're tuned into. My recommendation is to recognise someone's karma and say, "I choose not to go into that karma, my karma is going to be different. My behaviour is going to be different. Regardless of how much my ego thinks I'm justified in behaving the same way. I'm going to choose better and I'm going to send out the energy of love, forgiveness and prosperity, thereby attracting only love, forgiveness, prosperity."

That's why, when my clients come to my Mastermind, I focus on forgiveness at the beginning and it's a module that I keep referring to and keep sending them back to throughout the 12 months. We only cover vision boards in module 10. Why? Because my focus isn't on their material goals. My focus is to make sure their internal energy has shifted and changed. To make sure that they are now constantly in the energy of love and harmony and prosperity and forgiveness. Thereby attracting all this good stuff to themselves.

People want to manifest money and they want to manifest things, but they're holding on to grudges against exes, their bosses, their children, the parents and neighbours; you name it, they have it. People are angry about everything and anything or they're angry because something did this and someone else did that. You need to let it go, you can either be right, or you can be rich. You can be right and continue to hold on to the grudges, or you can choose to be rich and let them go. Now this is the caviar on top: keep in mind, just because you forgave somebody does not mean their karma has forgiven them. I don't hope, or want, or wish my ex to suffer the consequences of what he's done. Absolutely not. I wish him a world of happiness, I really do. I wish him all the happiness in the world. And I hope he gets a really loyal, loving partner. But whether he does or doesn't is between him and Divine Source Energy, I'm not interested in finding out. The problem is with these people, because they continue to behave in certain ways they'll have certain energies, the actions will create certain energies in their life, they will create the drama in their life again and again and again.

Going back to that saying that "Karma is a bitch; it always catches up with you." Karma isn't a bitch though; karma can only do what your energy is giving out. If someone's behaved in some way with you, they'll continue to behave in that way forever, or for as long as it takes until they change themselves. And if they do, they will attract all those things to themselves. You forgiving someone does not let them off the hook - the Divine Source Energy, or their karmic energy does not negate it because you've forgiven them.

You forgiving them does not negate the actions or let them off the hook from their karmic actions. It doesn't happen that way. This is one way to pacify your ego (lower self) by saying, "Look, I'm going to forgive this person. I'm going to wish them well. I really hope my ex has a really nice wife, and has a lovely family and he gets on, has all the happiness in the world." Whether he does or doesn't, it's up to him. It's his karma. The likelihood is from everything I know about karmic actions, for that to be true is unlikely, because I've let him off the hook, but Divine Source Energy will not. His karmic actions will have repercussions. One way to talk to your ego, in a way that will calm it down is to think "I'm letting this person off the hook. I don't know if Divine Source Energy will forgive him, I hope it does, but I don't know if it will. With everything I know about Divine Source Energy and about karmic actions, I doubt it. But I hope and I wish him well." Can we do that? If you talk like this to your ego, it takes the edge off and allows the ego to come into the mode of forgiveness. "OK I'll forgive him; I suppose he's not too bad. He's okay. I suppose. You know, do I wish him well? No, I really don't wish him well." You can have that inner dialogue with your ego. When you talk to your ego, it's almost like talking to a child. When I talk to my ego, I'll say, "Gull, it's okay, I know you're angry but okay, can we talk about this? It's okay. It's okay. Be kind to yourself. Be kind to your ego. Because remember, your ego is hurt. And your ego is justified in its anger and its frustration and annoyance." So you calm that child down, you calm that ego down and speak to it in a nice, kind manner and bring it to the point where you're able to forgive that person. Truly forgive - not superficially, but truly forgive that person or wish them well. Then you then let karma deal with everything else. It does, it doesn't, it's not your business. If you think, "Well, I'm going to forgive him and I'm going to wait to watch karma get his ass!" No, that's not you forgiving. That's you superficially forgiving, not forgiving truly, deeply and with all your energy. Say with your heart and mind and actually feeling, "I wish you well, I really would be happy to see you happy" that's what forgiving means.

Do I need to speak to the person physically to forgive them?

Now here's a question – do I need to talk to people who slander me? My opinion is, if someone's being rude or cruel to you, you can wish them well and disconnect energetically. There is nothing on the planet that says you have to see the people who have slandered you or your family or people who are mean to you. Do you have to be friends with them? Hell no. You have finite time on this planet. Can you understand this point? You have a finite amount of time. In that amount of time, why would I want to waste even a moment with people who are mean to me, cruel to me or slander me? I wouldn't waste any of those precious moments with people who do not value me. Instead, I'll forgive them and bless them for sure. I'll be nice to them if I see them, I'm always nice when I see people, but I will not associate with their energy, I will not be friends with them. I have moto: forgive all but forget nothing. I will make sure that I don't see them very often unless I'm going to family gatherings. I've got people in my family who are not very nice to me. Naturally, I have forgiven them, but I don't meet with them regularly. I don't associate with them regularly. It's my energy; I'm going to protect it. I don't want to intermingle with people who are not nice to me. But at the same time, I can bless them and be nice to them. All the while I protect, manage and value my energy so I do not give them my time. You can forgive them verbally out loud, or in your mind, or through energy and make sure you wish them well.

The Acid Test

This is the acid test. If you see them being happy and prosperous, are you happy for them? That's a hard thing to see when they have hurt you deeply. The acid test is when you've truly forgiven someone, you can see them being prosperous and happy and be happy for them. That's what you need to do. Not only do you need to forgive people for their actions, you need to forgive yourself for all the wrong actions you think you've taken, up until this point. You might think "Oh my goodness, I've been so horrible and so cruel." Wherever you were, allow it, just accept it. Be kind to yourself and know that you did the best you could with the knowledge you had, in the moment in time. You are where you are right now and you have what you have right now. It's not your fault. It's your social programming. It's the programming you received from the ages of zero to seven, you didn't know any better, it's as simple as that.

However, now you have received this knowledge through this book, therefore you now have the personal responsibility of changing your life from this day forward. If I've been bought into your world, there's a reason why. There's a saying I've mentioned previously; *"When the student is ready, the teacher appears."* If I've turned up in your life at this moment in time, and you are reading this book, this means I'm here to deliver a message and I'm here to guide you in a certain path. Take that on board and understand that this is from now, your responsibility to change your life. What happened in the past is not your fault as you were not aware of the laws or the subconscious programming. But from this day forward, it is your responsibility to change things – it is really important to do that, but start with forgiving and being nice to yourself. We are the harshest and most critical of ourselves. So be fair and be humble and be kind to yourself - you didn't know any better, you got to where you are. It doesn't matter what happened, you got where you are because of your social programming. From this day forward, you can change your life, you can move forward. This is where you need to go - this is what you need to do. It's vitally important that you are kind to yourself before and you are kind to others. Give yourself the same love and respect and blessings that you do to other people and remain in the energy of love and blessings towards yourself too.

What if you cannot avoid people who are cruel and mean, or maybe they are family members so you cannot totally ignore them? I see some of my family members when we have family gatherings once or twice a year? I see them; I smile at them and wish them well. I don't get into a conversation with them, I don't converse with them. I'm nice to them because you should not be rude to anyone. I'm always kind and nice to everybody. I smile and I say "Hello, how are you?" And that's the niceties done. That is it, a four word conversation and move on, next. Smile, say hello and move on. That's how you treat them. Wish them well.

That's a difficult thing. That's why when you spiritually evolve, it will become easier. The more you forgive people, the easier it will be to forgive people. The more you start forgiving people, the less people will turn up in your life that will need forgiveness   because remember, you only manifest what you give out. If you're forgiving and being kind to everybody all around, less and less people show up in your life which requires forgiving. That's the beauty of this.

Let's Recap:

We're at the end of another chapter, so now to recap that the third Law of Money is all about, the Law of Karma and the Law of Forgiveness. The Law of Karma dictates, regardless of what someone else is doing to you, YOU are fully responsible for your thoughts and actions and thereby your energetic vibration. The Law of Forgiveness says you need to forgive someone to such an extent that you bless them. Bless them completely and you wish them well and therefore you negate your bad karma, you don't actually have any bad karma towards them. If you don't forgive them, you retain the energy of negativity and anger, frustration and sadness, even if you don't act upon it. Even if you don't go out and physically cause them harm or physically slander them or physically do anything wrong to them, you still retain negative energy. Better to disconnect the negative energy you have, to issue the Law of Forgiveness, forgive them, bless them, and thereby you have negated your karma so you don't have any karmic action that way. You're only sending out good karma - good vibes, good positive   vibes. Be in a state of constant blessings and love. Therefore, what can the Universe reflect back to you? Love and blessings and that's it. Let's move on to the fourth law of money.

CHAPTER 7

THE FOURTH LAW OF MONEY
- THE LAW OF FAITH

"Believe in Your Heart
Believe in your heart that you're meant to live a life full of passion,
purpose, magic and miracles."

— **Roy T. Bennett,** *The Light in the Heart*

We are in chapter seven, and we are covering the fourth Law of Money, which is important yet is one of the most underused, underrated Laws of Money. It's just one of the Laws that fascinate me - which people ignore all the time.

Remember in the previous chapters I've talked about super-consciousness, subconscious and your conscious mind? Generally most people think the subconscious and your superconscious mind are one. I, on the other hand, think there's a third mind and that's a super-conscious mind and I'm not the only one - there are plenty of other authors and experts who say the same. The superconscious is actually the Divinity, the Divine Being in you that's present in every single individual.

Now there is religious background to that as well. All religious texts, all of them actually mention the concept e.g. The Old Testament says you are made in God's image, and in the Quran, it is stated that God is closer to you than the jugular vein. There's an element in all religions that talks about the fact that you are very, very close to God and God is very close, closer to you than anything else. All the great thinkers of our times have actually acknowledged the fact that Divinity exists in every single individual, that it is housed within me, within you; that's where you get the guidance, that's where you get the protection from.

For example, when you're walking out the door, and you're just about to cross the road when a fast car appears and you pull yourself back. You can say that that was your guardian angels, but I think that's your Divinity and it's telling you, "OK no, just wait half a second." Thus you prevent an accident. Or when you get gut feelings, your intuition basically, that is the house of the super-conscious.

Remember there are three components in your mind - your conscious mind, your subconscious mind and the superconscious mind. The superconscious is the one which is ignored the most.

Let's focus on the subconscious mind. The subconscious mind is responsible for your bodily actions and everything else that happens inside of you, but it's also responsible for the Law of Attraction, for the kind of chatter that goes on in your head, the energy of your mind, the kind of vibration you're at. Your subconscious mind actually determines the vibration you're actually vibrating at. Your level of vibration and the energy you're emitting to the outside world. Let's make this very, very clear. It doesn't have a mind of its own. The subconscious mind has been programmed between the ages of zero to seven by your primary caregivers and thereafter is taken care of by your external social programming. This will also have an impact on your subconscious mind. Most of the time, it creates self-fulfilling prophecies, a vicious cycle; you sort of expect some people to be a certain way in your life, and those people support your beliefs in those ideas. That's the subconscious mind, and the conscious mind is looking at reality as status quo. That's the house of the will. But now the superconscious mind: that is where the Divinity lives and that can actually bypass your subconscious programming. Now as I'm saying this, I know I'm going to be contradicting people who say, "Oh, no, this isn't how it works," but I'm here to tell you that's how miracles show up and I want you to start believing in miracles, I want you to expect things that are completely illogical, completely out of this world. That's the kind of expectation I want you to have. So the super conscious mind is where the Divinity resides, and it's what we use for this fourth Law of Money. Now, how do we use it?

Let me first explain what super consciousness is. Super consciousness gives you nudges; it's responsible for your intuition. But it's also responsible, at times, for bypassing the conscious mind when you connect with that part of your soul, when you connect with that desire. That desire coupled with faith is very important; it will actually reprogramme your subconscious mind for you, therefore attracting these things, without your will coming into it. A lot of the time, miracles are like that - I don't know how it happened, I didn't ask for this. And then it happened.

So the fourth Law of Money is the idea of you connecting with the superconscious mind that's part of you, the Divine part of you, and actually using that to create miracles.

How to Use Your Superconscious Mind to Create Miracles?

There comes a time when we are stuck between a rock and a hard place. You know, when you talk to God and say things like, "God, I'm done. I don't know what to do. I really don't know what I can do. I'm just really lost. Please just help me God, please just help me God". Have you ever reached that point? "Only God can help now, only God can help me with this, only God can do this." Every single one of us has gotten to that stage, when there's nothing else that you can logically do, and we have our backs against the wall   When we get to such dire states, when there is nothing left to do, that is when we FINALLY leave it up to GOD. Have you noticed when you do this, miracles show up? However, you don't need to hit rock bottom before you seek such miracles.

I call this casting the burden - when you just give away all the stress and anguish from that particular situation to God. "God, you deal with it, this is far too much for me, I cannot be dealing with it, here you take it, you deal with it." And that's when miracles show up. The person turns up with their deal, or the money comes through in time to fund a particular venture. Or your mother recovers, or your child recovers. Or your leg heals up, whatever; the miracles show up when you actually give up. Why does this happen? I'll tell you. There's a reason this only happens when you have no logical means to get where you want to go. You have no logical means to get to your desire. You're stuck with that, your hands are up, you're up against the wall, and you have no way to move forward. At that time, when your logical brain thinks there's nothing else I can possibly do, physically or emotionally. Therefore you cast the burden of that situation onto

God as a last resort. That's when miracles show up.

However, I'm telling you, you have access to this power, to this Divine power all the time. Usually you are using your willpower and your logical brain to get from point A to point B, but you often get stuck. Using money as an example, if you are currently earning, $2000 a month and you want to get to $20,000 a month, than your logical brain cannot comprehend how to get there, your subconscious mind might say, "Well, of course, we can't get that, we can't have that. It's not safe to do that." If you have not got your conscious and your subconscious mind to the level where you're capable of having that kind of money, you will not be able to get it. This is because there'll be a lot of resistance from your conscious and your subconscious mind. However, if you tuned into your superconscious mind and create a miracle for yourself, you will find that money shows up for you. The problem lies in the fact that, if your conscious and subconscious mind are not aligned with this amount of money, you will very quickly get rid of it. This happens a lot with people who win the lottery. However, miracles can and do show up. When you ask for that kind of miracle, miracles can show up for you.

So this is the fourth Law of Money. When you impress the superconscious mind, you expect miracles in your life and miracles do come in your life, for example - you win the lottery. But if your conscious mind and your subconscious mind are not there, if your money mindset is not there, your mental programming is not there, you lose the money.

We all have these examples where money just unexpectedly showed up. You thought to yourself, "Oh, my God, a miracle just happened. And I needed this money and the money just showed up. I don't know how it happened. I didn't know I had an aunt who died who gave me this inheritance."

Miracles happen because Divine Source Energy is always listening – it is omnipresent. We've actually used this intermittently every now and again, when we just really give up and think "OK, there's nothing I can do about it. There's nothing I can do apart from maybe God can do something. God showing me a miracle, please do a miracle." And a miracle shows up.

My whole point of this chapter is to actually use it as a Law of Money. Nobody else I know talks about this at all, about using or expecting miracles because it's illogical, and I'm a logical person, but I'm asking you to do something which is completely against logic, which completely goes against the conscious mind, which is where faith comes in. So how would you do this? As an example, if you want to go from $2,000 to $100,000 a month as a monthly income, what would you do? What would your steps be? Well, the first one is setting the goal of making $100,000 a month.

Secondly, would be to actually open up and start asking intuition. "OK intuition (Higher Self, God. Universe - whatever you want to call it is fine), what can I do? What business can I do? What can I set up so that I can make this kind of money? What can I do to actually have this kind of money?" That's the thing. But at the same time, you impress this onto your superconscious mind saying, "God, I want to earn this. And I don't know how to go from 2000 to 100,000, so I'm going put this burden on to you. Okay, I'm casting it onto you."

A lot of people do this, when it comes to emotional stress and other problems, people use this as a last resort. When they've given up, when everything that they've tried every resource possible, nothing else has worked so they fall back on "Only God can do this now." My question is, why do you leave it to the last moment? Why not simply cast this burden onto Divine Source Energy, and then keep holding the faith. Now faith is really important. The reason why miracles don't show up in your world, the reason why that $100,000 is eluding you, the reason why every time you think "OK, you know what, I'm going to set the goal of making $100,000 a month" yet nothing happens is this. You don't believe it. Fear steps in and it says, "Well you've never earned it before. Why would you earn it now?" and all that negative chitter chatter comes in.

I'm giving you a shortcut. I'm giving you access to the power that resides within your soul. The road from here to there is, you have to go through the subconscious mind, and you have to reprogramme your subconscious mind. I encourage you to do that anyway, I really encourage you to work on your money mindset daily. But today, this law specifically works where you just cast the burden on to Divine Source Energy and that superconscious mind of yours, you impress and say, "Look, God, I want $100,000 and I'm really working for it, I'm open to ideas that will allow me to have a business which will make me $100,000 and I'm holding the faith that you will show me the way where I can earn this money. Through my services, where I'm contributing to the world and to the betterment of the world to make the world a better place, through my services, and making $100,000 a month." We are actually impressing the superconscious mind, not just the subconscious mind. I know that there are a lot of books that talk about impressing the subconscious mind and getting the subconscious mind to work for you. Yes, all well and good. That's great. But the only way for you to attract things is through the superconscious mind. So that will direct your subconscious mind into lining up with energy, with people, with businesses.

Obviously, the subconscious mind will be used by the superconscious mind to get you to wherever you want to get to. But this law specifically works around impressing the superconscious mind with what you want, and holding on to the faith that you will definitely get it. Now, this works in every scenario, not just money. In health for instance, we've had people who've been told they'll be crippled for life, and they're walking around now. We've heard stories of people who've been told they have terminal cancer, and they're still alive, they've actually cured themselves. We know stories where people were told they can't have children, and now they have children. It works in every scenario, because we're used to hearing about miracles happening all the time. These miracles can show up in your daily life on a regular basis... if you permit yourself to have the courage to ask your superconscious mind. "Can I have this Divine Source Energy?" Whatever you want to call it - when I refer to Divine Source Energy, in my personal world, in my personal life, I would say Allah SWT, can I have this? Can we do this? Can I do this?" But depending on whatever your religion is, you can call it Rama, you can call it Jesus Christ, you can call it whatever term you want to give Divine Source Energy, it is entirely up to you. But use it and talk to Divine Source Energy. This is prayer with faith and expectation that it's going to be fulfilled.

"The world was made partly that there may be prayer; partly that our prayers might be answered."

— **C.S. Lewis**

Now, there's another point: a lot of people assume Divine Source Energy is somewhere out there - when you pray, you just automatically assume that you put your head down, or you look up. Divine Source Energy is everywhere. Let me repeat that, that is so important for you to understand this law. Divine Source Energy is everywhere. That includes you. Divine Source Energy is out there, over here, behind me, above me, below me and within me. That's why when you speak to Divine Source Energy you can converse very clearly because Divine Source Energy is in you too. It's inside every other individual, every living creature and therefore you can impress that mind. "God, I don't know how to go from 2000 to 10,000. Can you show me the way? Can you help me? Can you show me the path?"

That's impressing the superconscious mind. And then obviously, holding the faith. So, the biggest reason why miracles don't show up, is because every time your back is against the wall, you have this inner chatter, "Oh my God, this is going to happen, that's going to happen. This can happen." The fear comes in and whatever work you've done, whatever thing you've asked God to do for, you actually negate it. Because you think that's not going to show up. This is what happens a lot with people praying. A lot of people pray, pray, pray, but they're not expecting it. It's a prayer without faith or belief or expectation. They're not expecting the prayers to come to fruition. They're NOT expecting God to answer their prayers. If you are lacking in faith, you will not be given what you're asking for, as simple as that. Whatever your religious belief, irrespective of the name you give to Divine Source Energy, the Supreme Energy, Universal Energy, whatever you want to term it - if you are lacking faith, you will not be given what you're asking for.

So the fourth Law of Money is primarily having faith, asking Divine Source Energy by impressing the superconscious mind. "OK, you know what I want and Divine Source Energy, Allah Subhana Wa'Tala or Rama or Brahma... I want to go from $2,000 to $100,000 a month. I want you to show me the path. I want you to make a way for me. I'm casting the burden of this responsibility onto you. So now you find a way for me to make $100,000."

If you do this with faith, and that is the tricky part, if you do this with faith you will find that superconscious will actually trigger the connection to the subconscious mind, which will pass on some intuitive ideas to your conscious mind and say, "OK, go meet this person, try this business, do this, and do that." The path will be made for you and within a short period of time [and that's relative, depending on what you want - what do you call a short period of time], you'll be making $100,000 a month. But what was necessary in the first instance, you had to impress the superconscious mind. Not the subconscious mind, but rather the super-conscious mind, and then have faith.

When you ask for something from Divine Source Energy, pray not to God outside, but to the Divine Source Energy inside of you, your superconscious mind, and then hold onto faith. And when you hold the faith, you cast the burden, the responsibility of achieving this is now shifted. If you're at the point of saying "I'm so tired, I don't know how to deal with this situation. God, I can't deal with this. You know God, you deal with the situation now, I'm out, and I'm done. I'm done. I'm just helpless. I'm done." And we've all done this at times, right? When a situation becomes too big for us to deal with, we ask for miracles, and a miracle shows up. Because guess what, when things are really crap, we expect God to turn up and help us. That's typical, and the subconscious and the conscious mind don't interfere in that. We just think this is too big. Only God can help, and guess what? God helps, miracle show up. It's usually when we get to the end. When you're right at the end, you are no longer resisting. Remember the Law of Non-Resistance, you're no longer resisting anything. "There's nothing I can possibly do to help the situation. Only God can help." When you get to that point, when you activate the Law of Non-Resistance, you stop resisting the situation. God comes in, miracles happen and voila. When your back is up against the wall, you have no other options available, you give up and you say, "OK God, you take over, there's nothing else I can do." You activate the Law of Non-Resistance, and super-consciousness. And by doing that, in that moment, you have faith that God will help you.

Now this really does depend on how strong your faith in Divine Source Energy is. I keep reiterating this. However faith is something that's really important for this law. I highly recommend you go through the other chapters, to understand where we are. You'll know which direction I'm going in, but all of them will intertwine because in the this law in the end, we will put all the pieces of puzzle pieces together. Later in this book I'll tell you how to move forward. But this law is really important, it can only be activated when your back is against the wall and you stop resisting, whatever the situation you have at hand. When you stop resisting it, the Law of Non-Resistance comes into play. Then, obviously, the miracles show up because now you're actually using this fourth Law of money.

In short, the fourth Law of Money is pretty much faith – it's having faith when you ask Divine Source Energy to do something for you with that total utter 110% faith that it will be done. In effect, what you're doing is you ask something from God or from Divine Source Energy - which is within you, not something that's external, or outside of you. So you turn to the superconscious mind, God, higher self, Universe or whatever you want to term it. "I don't know how to do this. Can you help me? Can you show me a way?" With the 110% faith that it is going to be heard. The superconscious mind is going to listen to you and actually give you an answer. If the faith is lacking, you will not get there, you will not get an answer and you will be stuck where you are. For this law to be activated faith is required. You have to have faith that Divine Source Energy is going to listen to you, the superconscious part of you is going to listen to you, and give you a way forward. When you have that faith, what will happen is, your subconscious mind, with the necessary training and motivation, will give your conscious mind intuitive ideas of do this, do that, to get you to $100,000 a month.

Now, this can happen for smaller things as well. But the problem is, when you want to jump from $2000 to $10,000, your logical mind will interfere and you probably think "Yes, actually, I can do this." Your ego will interfere and say, "Well, you know what, it's okay, I know how to do this, I can find a way. Let me try this. And let me try that." It will try to find a logical way to get to your goal. However, it will be small steps in the direction of your small goal. This is where you start to lose momentum as it takes so long to get to even the smallest goals. When you set goals that are too low, your logical mind takes over to find a solution. When you set outrageous goals, goals that scare you yet excite you at the same time, you have no option but to use your superconscious and subconscious mind to achieve them as there is no logical way to get to them.

This is the reason why I love Bob Proctor; he talks about aiming too small. The reason why you don't achieve small goals is because you're aiming too low. When you aim low, your ego comes into play and it goes, "Oh, let me think I can do this. And I can do that". When your ego comes into play, you're playing small because you're logically working out how to go from this step to the next step.

When you are actually going for a massive goal, there's no logical way to go from $2000 to $200,000, there is no logical way, you have to use Divine inspiration, you have to work and tap into your genius, tap into something beyond your normal expectations or your normal ideas. This is why it's so powerful that you actually really do understand that you have a superconscious mind, which is always ready and listening to whatever it is that you want. Whatever your desires are, it will give them to you as long as you believe in it. Faith is essential for this law to work. Absolutely essential.

Let's recap:

So let's recap; we have three minds. Your three minds are your conscious mind, your subconscious mind and your superconscious mind. The fourth Law of Money is centred on your superconscious mind. That's the part of you which is Divine. It can also be called the Divine mind, the Divine Source Energy, that Source Energy within you, God in you, whatever you want to term it. That is the part that you ask and normally it only gets activated when your back is against the wall. When you think "There's no other way out." You don't know how else you're going to get help, you don't know where to get the help from, and usually that's when miracles show up. This is about expecting miracles. What I'm asking you to do is to use this law in your daily life for your normal daily goals, but also have large goals and say, "OK, I want x, y and z. I don't know how to get it, I'm leaving it up to you, I believe that you will show me the way and you will open up the path for me. I'm giving all the responsibility over to you. You deal with it". You'll find that when you do that, you actually feel relieved - it's like you literally are casting the burden, the headache, all the weight you're carrying on your shoulders for actually making this reality, you actually shift the burden. It really does do that, it shifts the burden of the desire onto Divine Source Energy and then miracles show up. Provided you have faith, miracles will show up. That's the fourth Law of Money.

CHAPTER 8

THE FIFTH LAW OF MONEY – THE LAW OF LOVE

*"When we show kindness to those who will repay us, it's called
'networking', when we show kindness with no thought of repayment,
it's called 'love'*

— **Dave Willis**

I know I always say this, I think all the laws that I talk about are all very vital, and are all very important when it comes to money. However, in this chapter I am going to discuss something really, really close to my heart... because I think my whole life is based on this law. It really is. Yes, I apply the Law of Forgiveness and I apply the Law of Karma and I have other things that I apply. But in totality my life is based on this law. One of the best compliments that I got was from somebody a while ago. They said that I'm the embodiment of this law, and when I talk about it, you'll understand what I mean.

It is something that I feel so strongly about; it is something that you should be practicing in life anyway. If you're not, I can guarantee you all the ills and all the problems – the root of the problems that you have, will have something to do with some aspect of this. It will be the violation of this law that will be one of the root causes for whatever's happening in your life. Any ills, anything that goes wrong, generally has a root cause based on the violation of this particular law. So what law am I talking about today? Why is it so important? And why do I love it so much? I mean, I just let the cat out of the bag there. The Law of Love.

The best and probably the most important law so far, is the Law of Love. Now before you ask, "Gull, what do you mean by this Law of Love?" If you look at Dr. David Hawkins and the spectrum of vibrations. I think it's a really great diagram in his book, Power vs Force, which shows the levels of vibrations for different emotions. The spectrum ranges from zero to 1000. Around 500 is love. Reaching 1000 is where you're a saint, you know, you're like Jesus, something like that. So the Law of Love is very, very important. Unfortunately very few people actually understand what love is.

We have this misguided and misunderstood myth of love and what love represents. What social media tells us, what the media tells us, what the films tell us love is. Unfortunately, most of the time they get it wrong. Generally what people think is that I need love to be okay. That's a very selfish concept. Whereas love itself is very selfless. That is why sometimes people say that the mother's love is truly selfless. That's a true embodiment of love. The best compliment that I got from a friend of mine, and it was quite shocking, was when he told me that I was the embodiment of love. Because I approach everything from the element of love. How can I give love to this? How can I do this? If you get this law, if you really understand this Law of Love, I guarantee you everything, forgiving people will be easier, forgiving yourself will be easier and manifesting things will be easier. Everything becomes easy. The application of all other laws becomes really, really easy, even the Law of Word. You speak better when you embody love. Every other law, the application of every other law becomes really easy when you understand this Law of Love. Unfortunately, many people get it wrong.

Now, let's start from the beginning. What do I mean when I talk about love? Love is a cosmic phenomenon that opens up the fourth dimension for humans, for men, and for women. As people, we live in the third dimension, but when we actually truly love somebody or something, it actually opens up the fourth dimension. It opens up the world of wonders. It really, really does. Real love is selfless. And it's free from fear. Unfortunately, most of the time when we love, including as parents, we're worried about what's going on, what's going to happen, what's going to happen with the children, will our children love us back and so forth. Unfortunately, the kind of love that we as people are used to in this day and age is very, very selfish. Real love is actually selfless.

This is what you need to embody. And by the way, I am a work in progress. For example, I got my daughter's school report yesterday, and it wasn't what I expected. I was really upset with her, and I had to stop myself. Afterwards I calmed down and realised, and I do tell her this, my love is unconditional, but I was annoyed because it kept saying she's very able, but she's being lazy. I'm telling you this and I'm saying this is what I truly try to live by, but I'm still a work in progress. Despite being socially conditioned to think of love in a particular way. Real Love is selfless and free from fear. It pours out of your heart, literally out of your heart upon the object of your affection, whether it is your child, your pet, your house, your car, whatever it is.

It could be an inanimate object, like a car or a house, or it could be organic like a living creature, a human being, your child, your spouse, your friend, or a pet or an animal. But the key point is, it doesn't demand anything in return. The joy is the joy of giving.

Yet very few people truly understand this point. Love is like God in manifestation. It's the strongest magnetic force in the Universe. It really is. If you truly, truly love someone, you do it unselfishly and you give love out. So you give out love for the sake of love. I want you to really understand this point, when you're giving love out for anything, and I will explain to you how this is relevant for money in a bit. But when you give love out for the sake of love, right, just the sake of giving, you are not expecting anything in return. As an example, let's say you love this person, this guy, or a girl that you really think is adorable or a spouse, you really love. You give them unconditional love, and they either pass away or they leave you or something happens, and they don't reciprocate your love. You are not loving them for them to love you back. You're loving them for the sake of loving.

If your love is pure and true and sincere, what will happen is, somebody else will love you back. You will get your love back; you can only receive what you give out. If you give out true unconditional love that is what will come back to you. Remember; whatever you get back is what you've given in the first place, right? So this love will come back to you. It may not be from that person, it may be from an alternative source, but you will get love back. When you have this selfish idea that I'm giving this, and I'm giving that because I need to get something in return, that's exchange, that's not love. I really want to clarify this. When you say I will love you if you do x y and z [and as parents we do this as well], I will love you if you do this, that's an exchange, that's the barter system. That's not love. Love is unconditional and love is truly without expecting anything back. Purely loving for the sake of loving.

True love doesn't demand anything or seek anything. Unfortunately as humans, as people we are fearful, we are selfish. We're so afraid of losing the thing we love because "Oh my god it's going to cause us so much pain." We actually try to hold on to it really, really tightly, don't we? For example if we love anything, we end up being jealous, that's when jealousy is born. But jealousy is the worst enemy of love. It really is. Because if you're jealous you picture all sorts of funny things in your mind. Remember the Law of Attraction. If you're imagining things in your mind and you are emotionalising it because you get upset and annoyed about those pictures, then obviously they will materialise in your external world - that's how manifestation works. But if you love someone or you love something without any fear, and that can only be if you no longer hold on to desiring, then that is loving for the sake of love. When you love something without any expectation of getting anything back at all, when there's no fear involved - that is a purest form of love. Now, how many people do you know who love from that pure energy? Mother Teresa? Princess Diana is another example. There are many examples like that; people will love them when they embody love like that.

What are you exuding? Love? What can you possibly get back but love? When you give out perfect love you will receive perfect love. Let's just get that right. Perfect love is unselfish and not demanding. It does not criticise your content. Just bless your loved ones. When you send out real love, that's when you receive it – it will return to you many fold. I want to bring this home for a few reasons. This applies in a business situation or a personal situation, I'm not just talking about romantic love here. I'm talking about love in general. This love is for your business partners. This love is love for your neighbours, love for your parents, love your children, love for your friends, including spouses and boyfriends and girlfriends and romantic love. But I'm talking about all sorts of love.

Unfortunately, humans are selfish. Therefore when they do love someone, they demand that love be given back. If it isn't, they take the love away. That's the barter system and it's not what we want. There's an old saying that *"No man is your enemy. And no man is your friend. Every man is your teacher."* This is so important to know. When you really love someone, and they misbehave with us, or actually treat us nicely, they are teachers and they are teaching us the lesson in some way. When you become free from the want of needing people's love, of needing people's approval, you become free.

Now how does this tie in with money? Well, we need to treat money as your best friend. You need to have a love of money. I've talked about this time and time and time again. You can probably feel my energy when you hear me say I love and respect money. Because I think money is amazing. You can do some amazing things with it. But I have great admiration, respect and love for money. Regardless of how much money shows up in your bank account. I want to make this clear. I love money regardless of how much shows up in my bank account. If there's one pound in my bank account, or a thousand, or a million, I love money the same amount - that hasn't changed. I'm not expecting money to give me anything in return, money is just money. It is just a form of energy and I love and respect it.

Can you see the difference?

Usually what people have is they have the <u>greed</u> of money rather than the love of money. The greed of money gets them fearful and starts them hoarding and saving. Unfortunately all the biblical and religious texts talk about the greed of money, in the form of *'When the love of money takes over you actually end up causing more harm because not only is it the root of all evil, it causes a man's destruction and the money will eventually leave.'* Anytime you want to try and hold onto something like this: "Don't go, don't leave me". When you have a fear of losing it, that thing or a person or object will eventually leave you - it's the law. But when you have this unconditional love for something without the fear of losing it the way I've just described, money cannot help but love you back. Remember you can only get back what you give out. I'm giving out this love and respect for money and that's why I spend all my time learning about it, studying it, teaching people about money because I know how important it is and how valuable it is and what good money as a tool can be used for. I am giving out this love for money, and what I can receive back is the love and admiration and that's where money comes to me very easily. I respect it but you know there's also that element of understanding, so I understand the Laws of Money. I understand that money has to flow, that means to come in and flow to me then through me to other places like my utility bills, my other business expenses and obviously spending money on my family and whatever else. So money flows through me, not to me. My love for money is to such a great extent that I respect it when it comes to me and I respect it when it goes out.

I don't think very many people understand how vitally important this is - the love for something without the greed for something.

Unfortunately, most of the time we as people, we actually become very greedy. If you're attached to something then you just want it to be yours all yours. How does this help you with money? Two ways. First of all, when you have love for something, when you come from a place of love your vibration naturally raises. You naturally raise your vibration and therefore you attract more opportunities and circumstances and ideas to make money. Money comes to you in a greater abundance. Secondly and more importantly what you'll find is, not only do you attract money but you attract abundance in all forms, abundance in your health, wealth and relationships.

Remember I mean abundance in the greatest scale of things, I mean abundance in relationships and abundance in health, abundance in money and not only that, for money to bring you abundance of happiness. Money comes to me in large amounts but it comes in waves. I am happy, my clients are happy, my children are happy, my friends are happy - there's a lot of happiness around here and this is where love comes in.

Because a love for money is distinctly different from the greed of money, and I really want you to get this. The love for money is completely distinct and different from the greed of money. Most people - I think 99.9% of people - when they really start loving money, they start loving it with the greed of money not with the respect of money and this is unfortunately the problem. A lot of people say, "Well you know money isn't important; I just want to be happy." Somewhere along the way people have made loving money and respecting money synonymous with greed and arrogance. And they believed it to be mutually exclusive from happiness and joy. Therefore if you want money, you cannot want happiness or love.

Money is seen to be awful,   so disgusting, evil and dirty that if you love money then you don't want to be happy. If you love money then you don't want to be faithful, if you love money you can't be kind, if you love money you can't be an honest person.

That's the kind of image we have and this is where that negative programming comes in. The kind of image that social media gives us, and other places, you know if you desire money, if you talk about money you must be a horrible person right? This is the point. Your love for money has to be quite distinct from the greed of money and if you're saying I don't want money, I can't have money, money is not important to me, what will you attract?

I see a lot of struggling artists - they don't want money, "Oh I just love music, I love my thing, my art, I'm not really bothered about money, I don't really care about money." Those people will not have money! When it comes to people that have no money, I often see their disrespect and disregard and this hatred or almost aversion to money. This is why this fifth Law of Money is so important - the love of money and I truly mean it with all sincerity - for you to get money, you need to fall in love with money. Not falling in love in the greedy way, not like "When it comes to me let me hoard it, let me hoard every single penny." I've seen people like that; I've seen people who are financially wealthy but are very poor. Poor rich people, I've seen plenty of those. There's a family that comes to mind - they've saved every single penny over a number of years and then they invested in that second house and the third house - they've got three or four properties so they are millionaires, wealthy but they like to hoard the money. They're very poor in mind and in heart. They're not very giving, they're not very generous at all. That is not true wealth to me and that remember, takes years as well. There are plenty of ways to make money but when you come from the element of loving money you attract it to you. So you activate this law which allows money to love you back and therefore come to you in larger and larger amounts and stay with you for longer and longer duration. This is so powerful, so simple yet so misunderstood.

Love money for the sake of loving - do not love it so that it comes into your bank account. I love money now and my love for money now will not be any different to when I have a million bucks in my account. That is not going to change. Love for the sake of loving. This is almost like a shortcut, cutting across all the B.S. that you have learned about money. Love money for the sake of loving. It doesn't matter how much of it comes to you and when it comes to you allow it to flow through you. I always talk about treating money as your best friend – treat it as someone who comes and you welcome them with open arms but when they need to go, you let them go. You're happy to receive them and you're happy to let them go. That is also something you need to do with money.

There is ebb and flow of money and you need to accept and respect this principle, This principle is even more important. You need to be best friends with money AND allow it the freedom to come and go as it need. Your utility bills, your business bills, your investments, wherever. When you activate this Law of Love you literally create miracles all the time. By the way you can activate this law for anything - for relationships, for your health - I mean all the laws that I've talked about are applicable to any manifestation at all. In manifesting anything from a partner to health to whatever. I specifically use it in the context of money because I think money is the most misunderstood concept there is out there. Therefore, you activate this law when you actually fall in love with money for the sake of loving, not because you want it, not because you want to hoard it, not because you want to keep it in your pocket. Not for that. That is when money starts coming to you in huge quantities, it really does. By the way this is a really, really important thing to remember. If you love someone... really, really love them with all your heart, that person will pick it up on a subliminal level, on a supernatural level and may not actually reciprocate it as much as you would like for whatever reason but they will reciprocate it. This is a fact. If I go into a room and there's someone who's attracted to me, I will pick it up. It's called your intuition. I will pick it up - I may not reciprocate it but I'm aware of it and there's a little part of me which is [depending on how strong the attraction is]. I've seen this happen time and time again when somebody truly loves another person [it has to be true love by the way] that love is reciprocated, to some extent. If that person doesn't return the love, love will come from somewhere else. I do believe that. That's just how the Divine Universal Laws work. In the context of money, love money and respect money in the way I'm teaching you at the moment and if you do it unconditionally so you love money for the sake of loving... you love and respect money for the sake of loving and respecting it, not so that you can have something, not so that it will come to you, not so that it comes and stays in your bank account - you just love for the sake of loving, without any conditions without any hooks, without any preconceived ideas of what money is. Money will come to you because of what you're sending out - you're sending out this love and high vibration for money, therefore money has to come back to you. Does that make sense?

This is one of the simplest things you can do and this will also sidestep your subliminal programming that you've taken on about the negative ideas about money. When we start loving money in this way, if you love someone truly then you don't listen to the rubbish about them. That's another one to think about for a second - if you are truly madly in love with somebody I could say anything about them and you would say "No that's not true. I know she's not like that. I know he's not like that." Can you do that for money? Can you actually do that? Can you actually love money like that so that it doesn't matter what the media says? By the way I'm like that, so when I'm sitting there and I can honestly say this - when I'm sitting on my sofa and somebody comes up with rubbish about money, especially when watching Netflix or one of these stupid programmes, you know these social dramas, I love to say, "I know that's not true about money." I would actually defend it, I will defend money. I'm defending money because my children watch me. I'm setting the example for my children. I'm telling my children, "Look, this is what they want to say about money. Look at that, how they're wrong." Anything negative or derogative about money, I will reject it and vocalise my rejection. I'll defend money. Can you understand that? If you can't, then that's something that you have to learn to do. Because that's where you need to be when you start loving money like this. I have regular conversations with money through my money Avatar. I ask money "Where do you want to go?" And a lot of the time, you'll find that money will tell you where it needs to go. If somebody needs it. Of course you need to have a residence. But if money needs to go towards a charity, you give it to that charity; if it goes towards your family, you know, give it to your family. If money needs to be spent on your own self, buy a new dress or an outfit or something else.

Buy that. Let money flow, keep the circulation going, and don't hold on to money. Of course, be wise with money and I would highly recommend you get financial advice and invest and save. Absolutely. But don't hoard it; don't have the greed for it. This fear that if money comes to you, you'd better hold onto it because you might lose it – that is a fear that you need to eliminate. And the best way to eliminate any fear of losing is to love without wanting. That's so powerful. Think about that for a moment. When you have no fear of losing money, you can just love it without any conditions attached – unconditional love - that is when money will start coming to you in such large quantities, it will blow your mind.

Let's Recap:

I hope today's chapter was useful to you. I live my entire life on this premise that I come from a space of love for everything. Yes, I'm human. And yes, I'll have a reaction every now and again. But generally I come from a space of love. Okay, I will love you, I will send you blessings and then I'll let you be. And I may not have time for someone, as you make time for those who are important to you. However you can send love and blessings to all. I always believe that there's this small amount of time that we are on this planet. Therefore I may not give someone my physical time anymore; I may keep my distance from them too. However, I would love them and I will bless them and I will let them be. I learn my lessons and move on. I come from a space of love. And when you do that, you love for the sake of loving, not for expectations, not for anything in return. Because when you are expecting things you are bartering.

True real love is unconditional loving. And that is what I want you to have - this true unconditional love for money. Because money deserves it. Money is energy. It's amazing. It can do so many good things for you. It deserves to be loved. And it's not selfish. Money is neutral - you decide what you want to use it for, good or bad, money doesn't decide for you. Therefore if you can respect, love and have that admiration for money, then money can come to you in large quantities.

I really, really hope you can and this may sound challenging to some people, it may sound superficial to other people. I can own up and say I truly love and respect money unconditionally. It comes in, it flows through me to wherever it needs to go. Some of the money does go into investments, some money does go into savings because I'm wise and I use financial principles. But when it comes, it goes. Because I know more of it will come. There's no fear attached to it. I'm no longer afraid of money not coming. I'm no longer fearful that money will run out. Money comes, money goes. I love and respect money unconditionally and after reading this chapter, I hope you will too.

CHAPTER 9

THE SIXTH LAW OF MONEY
– THE LAW OF INTUITION

"Intuition is a very powerful thing, more powerful than intellect, in my opinion."

– Steve Jobs

We're on chapter nine and today we are talking about the sixth Law of Money. We're going to talk about intuition and the right guidance. Now what do I mean by intuition? Intuition is not something that you logically come to. A lot of the time this is your hunch, your gut feeling, or something that you just know you need to do without even having a solid reason for why. It comes in different forms. Intuition can come in the form of a question such as "So how do I deal with this issue?" When you ask God for a sign or when you just ask a question like, "How am I supposed to do this?"

You're thinking about an issue and the solution to that problem or the answer to that question pops up either on the radio, or it pops up as you're reading a book or nowadays in social media, you're looking through Facebook or Instagram and the message appears for you.

You know internally, "This is a message for me. It's been given to me by Divine Source Energy and it's my reply to the question that I was asking". That is what happens when you have intuition. Now that is generally what people are familiar with. However, a lot of times, as you start using your intuition more and more, what you find is that you actually begin to hear more and see more signs. You get to hear things in your head or have this feeling, and usually when the answer's given, especially when you have a feeling, it's illogical. I'll give you an example. I'm very intuitive, and I'm currently doing a Challenge with one of my groups. In that group, I gave them a task of repeating three lines of text one after the other. However, when I was giving the task, I heard very clearly in my head. "No, only give them the first line". That was the message. Now because I am so in tune with my intuition, I can hear things very quickly and I act on it. I don't question it. That's what happens when you start actually understanding and applying the laws of your intuition.

This is the Law of Intuition or the Law of Right Action. Actually you can call it either. 'Right' being the operative word here. You find that when you get used to it, you don't question the instructions given. On the face of it, logically, it makes no sense for you to have those instructions. But when you follow through and look back in hindsight, you realise, "Oh my goodness, that was the perfect thing for me to do at that time". You actually end up being at the perfect place at the perfect time doing the perfect action. That's what intuition is. It can come in any form and the more you cultivate it and use it, like a muscle, the better it gets.

"Intuition does not come to an unprepared mind."
— **Albert Einstein**

The more you use your intuition the sharper your intuition will become and the more you can act on it. Now, why does that happen? Well, let me just go a bit 'woo' on you. Your guides and angels and Divine Source Energy are always present. So they're constantly giving you guidance, advice and instructions. The problem is not their advice or help or guidance. The problem is your ability to listen and understand what's going on. Intuition is like a muscle in that, the more you use your intuition, the sharper your inner senses become, and you are able to listen and hear and understand better.

It's your ability to listen and understand the advice being given, that improves, not their messages. Let me make that very clear. As you act on your intuition, as you focus and develop your intuition, it's not their guidance that improves because that's always constant and it's always there. It's your ability to act upon it, it's your ability to listen to it, and it's your ability to manoeuvre through it. That's what intuition is. Your guidance is given to you and obviously the guidance is given in the best way that you'll be able to understand. So it's given in the language that you can understand. And I always say this, for example, if you speak Spanish, there's no point in me giving you instructions in Japanese, because you're not going to understand Japanese, you need to understand in Spanish. In the same way, whatever medium is suited to you and who you are and what you can understand in this physical body, that's how your intuition will guide you. Remember, you'll have your limitations being in this physical body. Those are the certain parameters that your guides and angels will use to communicate with you.

"There is a voice that doesn't use words. Listen."

— Anonymous

They will not come and communicate with you in French, if you don't understand French. However, if French is your first language and you're French, of course that's the primary language they're communicating with you, be it through written format or through the audio or whatever it is. Does it make sense? Really important for you to understand that your guidance is always constant. All the guides and angels are always constantly there to help you, to give you advice because Divine Source Energy doesn't favour one person over the other. Every single leader in history, every single person who's accomplished anything in our modern day world will tell you if you go and speak to them, that they all rely on their intuition in one form or the other. They may not call it 'intuition', they may call it 'a hunch', they might call it 'my gut feeling', whatever. But if you actually break it down, get rid of all the terminology that they use, at the core is actually intuition. It's them seeking and acting on the guidance that was given to them through these guides and angels, which is ultimately guidance from Divine source Energy.

Now, if you want to do this on your own and not use the advice from the higher power, if you want to gain money on your own, you're absolutely welcome to do so, but it's a long walk towards the path of prosperity and it's an uphill struggle. You're literally picking up a boulder and you're climbing and taking it with you up a hill, it's that heavy. On the other hand if you start listening to your intuition, what you'll find is that you are given shortcuts and opportunities and things will just line up.

You find yourself at the right place at the right time meeting the right people, doing and saying the right thing. That's why your prosperity opens up. This is why your intuition is absolutely key. Now more than intuition, is the right action. I'm going to say this again, more than intuition, is the right action. Because not only do you have to listen, your intuition is you being able to listen, to be able to understand and decipher what's being said to you, what guidance is given to you, that's intuition. The 'right action' is actually you implementing that intuition, actually acting based on that intuition, that is even more important.

Let me give you another example. There are many instances when Divine Source Energy wants to develop or further the physical world. In this case four or five people will receive the same intuitive message. For example, the idea of the modern phone and light bulb and every other major invention. This wasn't just given to Thomas Edison. That intuition must have been given to at least four or five other people, but only Thomas Edison put the effort and time into making it happen. The Wright brothers may have flown the first airplane, but they weren't the only people who were given the intuition, the guidance to do this, but they were the ones to act upon it. Nature rewards those who take the right action. Now keep in mind; I'm talking about the right action. Not wrong action. A lot of people just chase their tail taking wrong action and they think, "Well, I'm taking all the action, I'm being really busy and I'm doing all this work and I'm not getting results".

You may be busy and taking lots of action. You may not be productive because you're not taking the right action. Does that make sense? I'm here to tell you, you have to take the right action, based on your intuition, to be able to get to that pot of gold a lot quicker. The pot of gold exists, it absolutely does, but you have to take the right action in order to get there. So that's why this law is so important. You can't let go of this, because absolutely you have to take action. I'm not the type of person who says, "Oh, you sit in a room and chant affirmations all day and a bag full of money falls into your lap", absolutely not.

I do talk about surrender. If you've read these chapters in order there's a reason why I've given these laws in this order. Because you have to first surrender, you have to apply the Law of Love, you have to apply the Law of Word. You have to do that. You have to first believe what you are asking for is going to happen and then you have to open yourself up to receiving messages and guidance on how to take the right action to get to where you need to go to manifest, whatever it is you're asking for. This action is important but it comes after all the other rules. Without it you will not receive what you're asking for because whatever you want is already present in your abundance warehouse.

Whatever you want is already present in your abundance warehouse but taking the right action will allow it to manifest, and 'manifest' really means it's going from the spiritual world into the 3D world. You absolutely do need to take the right action in order to manifest what you want.

You have to take the right action to take the desire from the spiritual world and bring it into the 3D physical world. Intuition is a muscle that you absolutely can practice with and improve and sharpen over time. And as I say again, it's not based on what guidance has been received – it is what guidance you're actually able to interpret, listen to, hear, and act on.

The sixth Law of Money is all about the Law of Intuition or the Law of Right Guidance or the Law of Divine Guidance. This all translates into the Law of Right Action, because you need to take action on it.

Why is intuition so important?

Now why is intuition so important? Intuition is so important because it will give you shortcuts to your desired destinations, be it wealth, health or relationship goals. However, the messages can be quite startling when you first hear them - but you have to act and you have to take action without hesitation.

If you get guidance on, for example, you need to write a book, then you need to write a book there and then. If you have been told to maybe go to a coffee shop and you hadn't planned to go to a coffee shop, but you ended up going anyway because *you're listening*, and you meet a friend who needs your help. That's Divine Guidance. That's the right action. Even though it wasn't in your plan, it wasn't in the diary to go to the coffee shop today; you were guided to go there. You go anyway and you meet this friend and you end up helping him with whatever problem he has. So this is why you have to act - don't hesitate, or it could be you meet somebody who is able to find a solution for you or help you with a solution to whatever problem you have which you've been struggling with for the last two weeks.

Things like that happen all the time. I don't have to tell you this. You are familiar with it. But you should act swiftly and without hesitation. Remember this; your intuition will never explain to you the reason why it's asking to do certain things. It never tells you why you're doing this, it just tells you <u>to do</u> it. It's only when you take action and you look back in hindsight, you realise how everything just lined up and everything just perfectly came together in the end. Now let me also mention something dangerous. Unfortunately, with the rise of New Thought or New Age or Scientology or whatever else, unfortunately there's a huge number of people who now rely on the science of numbers, horoscopes, and other things.

The problem with those things is, and I'm not discouraging you from them, I think they can be very entertaining and I'm able to look some of them up and you take them for guidance, but I know when to take the guidance because my intuition is quite sharp. Most people misinterpret them. I'm going to repeat this again. Most people misinterpret the signs and symbols and therefore they end up giving the wrong prophecies to people. I never go to guidance on numbers. I never go to guidance on a dream or horoscope because I know the fact that whatever somebody's saying, they are actually prophesising for me and if I believe that that's going to happen, it will happen. So when somebody tells you that this is going to happen in your life or that's going to happen in life, you end up employing the Law of Prophecy. Or the Law of expectancy and therefore you start expecting that bad things are going to happen.

I'm quite intuitive and I do see things and I'm one of those people who actually sees symbols, I see signs, I see situations. Because I'm so highly intuitive I sometimes can see into the future, and see what's going to happen, I get premonitions. I'm one of those select few who do get premonitions. Now I can see good things and bad things. I never ever tell somebody about the bad ones. I may give them guidance on how to, because that particular scenario may not happen. I'm seeing it because there are a lot of life paths here so I give them advice and guidance on how to manoeuvre away from it. I don't tell them about it, as it maybe that it was only a path open for them and by telling them about it, I planted the seed in their mind and now they are EXPECTING it to happen.

Remember I did psychic work for a while on a telephone site. I was a telephone psychic for a few months. When I was first starting out as an intuitive and I was practicing my skills, I found working as a psychic was a great way to practice. It helped me to get very good. I'm generally very, very good and my accuracy rate is about 80 to 90%, I'm pretty accurate most of the time. However, the problem is, when you go to psychics, even though they could be wrong, you're trusting their intuition rather than your own. If you are seeing symbols, if you are seeing numbers, trust your own intuition to interpret it for you. Remember, your guidance is specific to you. Only you can know what it means for you.

For instance you might see the number 333 or 11:11. Trust your own intuition to understand what it means. Don't rely on somebody else. I think there's too much reliance on "What do you think about this?" and "How do you see this?" and whatever else. The Law of Intuition dictates that all the guidance that you need or will ever have a desire for is given <u>directly to you</u>. There is no other medium. There is no need to use another medium because the Divine Source Energy and your guides and angels will communicate with you in the way that you will hear best.

If it's through writing, it will show you in writing. If it's through audio, you probably hear it on the radio or your friends will say it, or somebody else will say it. If it's through visuals, you'll probably see it on the TV, or social media, or Instagram or somewhere. Your guides and angels will communicate with you what they need to, in order to get the message across to you through the medium that you understand best. You rely on your own guidance, not on somebody else's. I hope I'm making it clear. I'm not against psychics, again I'm psychic myself. I'm against these psychic sites. These sites keep giving you a lot of BS so that you keep returning for more. You become a repeat customer. Also, when I was working on such sites, I came to the conclusion that a lot of people who call such sites are not actually looking for the truth. They want you to tell them what they want to hear. If you spoke the truth, some people got very upset.

I want you to start to become self-reliant and the way to be free - to become self-reliant - is to train your intuition muscles. Start listening, hearing and whenever you get a message and you have this feeling in your gut like, "This is for me, this is the answer for me" for a split second you will get that feeling, accept it and ACT upon the guidance. Whether you dismiss it is another thing altogether but you will get a feeling for that split second, "That is the answer to that question I was asking". And that's the beauty of intuition.

Now how to cultivate intuition? That's the one thing that I think everyone asks me, so how do we go about cultivating it? How do we improve our intuition? Great question. I'm here to answer that for you. So the best way to actually improve your intuition and develop your intuition is through meditation. You can't get away from it. You need to silence your chitter chatter and your normal mind.

There is too much noise going on through Facebook and TV and your family life drama, your work drama, neighbours and whatever else. The best time to actually slow everything down and listen to your intuition is first thing in the morning or last thing at night. You need to close your ears to all the rubbish, all the chatter, all the noise that's going on around you and actually sit down and just be with yourself, your higher self and Divine Source Energy.

I recommend, if you are not used to meditating, then get some meditation tracks. I have a meditation which I think is really, really powerful, which is 'The Millionaire in the Mirror'. If you want to email us, someone from the team will send you a link for it. You can also go on YouTube, there are plenty of meditative sounds there. Dr. Joe Dispenza has a free meditation on YouTube and it's about becoming nothingness. That's a great meditation as well. There are plenty of meditations out there, guided meditations to use from these sites, but pick one that resonates with you and do it consistently and regularly every single day at the same time. My recommendation is early morning or last thing at night. When I say 'early morning', the best time to meditate is between four and six in the morning. In the evening, whatever time before you get to bed.

Why between four and six in the morning? Because before four and six in the morning, everything is very quiet. That's also called Sattvic Time. Well, Sattvic Time starts slightly earlier. Sattvic Time is from about 3:00 AM onwards, but it's a really, really powerful time and that's the time when you are actually really highly in tune with your higher self and it's easier for you to gain insights and get intuitive guidance in terms of what your next step should be. You don't have to think of the problem, you just have to just be there. Empty your mind. Now people say, "Oh, well, when I do meditation all these thoughts come to mind". That's okay, that's fine. Allow your mind to bring the thought to the forefront. Accept it, honour it, and then let it go and just keep your focus on your breath. I'm not going to teach you meditation. There is plenty of guidance out there. I'm not going to cover it in this book. In this chapter I'm telling you about the sixth Law of Money, which is all about Divine Guidance, taking Divine Guidance and then taking right action.

Just taking action on its own will not bring prosperity to you, it really will not. This is why I love the book 'The Science of Getting Rich' because Wallace D. Wattles talks in there quite clearly that getting rich is not by doing the actions. You get rich by thinking in a certain way. Thinking in a certain way and then taking actions accordingly. That's how you get rich, and that's really one of the most important laws. I think all of the laws are very important but this is one of the laws that a lot of people miss. People either act or they seek guidance but they don't do both.

Let's recap:

The sixth Law of Money, is the Law of Divine Guidance or the Law of Intuition. Taking the Divine action based on the information. It is really important that you are actually taking the right action. I've also explained to you that the best way for you to actually cultivate and develop your intuition is through meditation.

There's no getting around it. I'm going to give you another example. This morning I was running a Challenge in my group and that's quite intense because I'm connected to every single person's energy and I'm making sure I personally reply to all the comments and I'm going back and communicating and having conversations with all these people in the group.. That's a lot of work and taking their energy, at the same time I'm also preparing for the conference we're doing in Maldives. Both of these works are really stressful.

They're taking a lot of my time and so when I got up this morning I was extremely tired and all I wanted to do was go back to bed, I kid you not. At six in the morning, and that's actually late for me - I normally wake up at four. I woke up at six o'clock and I still wanted to go back to bed. So I dropped my son off to school in the morning because he had a morning club and then I came back and I thought I had two options: I could take a nap or I could do a meditation.

Guess which one I chose? Meditation. So I thought, "OK, I'm not going to take a nap for an hour, let me do meditation for an hour instead." I kid you not, once I did my meditation I felt alive and revitalised and clear and happy and I was just so together. There was an absence of stress, no pressure. Yes, I had a lot of things to do and I ticked them off one by one. Done, done, done, which is great, but there was no stress because of that meditation. And because I've done the meditation I know for a fact that I'm taking Divine action.

I'm not just acting for the sake of it. Any action I'm taking, I'm Divinely guided to "Do this call and then do that call" and I'm doing it. Done, done, done, and it works. I think meditation is something very personal, you can do it yourself or you can use guided Meditations and there are plenty of guided meditations on YouTube. If you want my one, which is 'The Millionaire in The Mirror', which is a very powerful one, drop us an email and we can send you the link for it.

I hope you got value from this chapter, which is all about the sixth Law of Money. Let's cover the final law of money in the next chapter.

CHAPTER 10

THE SEVENTH LAW OF MONEY
– THE LAW OF DIVINE DESIGN

"Give me the wisdom to know what to do and the courage to do it"

— Anonymous

Welcome, we're here with the final chapter with the seventh Law of Money. It will probably put everything together for you. We've covered six laws. In this chapter, I'm going to cover the seventh law, and you'll understand why this is the seventh and why the laws were given in this order.

The seventh Law of Money is called The Divine Design. Now this is based on the idea that every single person on the planet is born with a different Divine Design, the Divine Source Energy has a particular design and a particular purpose for every single person, every single soul. Think about this - if you look at snowflakes, there are hundreds and thousands of millions of snowflakes. Yet no two snowflakes are alike. If that's true about snowflakes, imagine yourself! Imagine you, your soul, the energy of who you are. This is the beauty of Divine

Design. Every single one of us has a particular design, a particular purpose that only you can fulfil.

"Everyone has a purpose in life... a unique gift or special talent to give to others. And when we blend this unique talent with service to others, we experience the ecstasy and exultation of our own spirit, which is the ultimate goal of goals." – Deepak Chopra

Not only is that wonderful, and it helps to build up your self-belief and your self-worth. It also gives a reassurance that you're here for a purpose. You're not just here to bounce off the walls and fill up your pockets with money and eat food and go to the toilet and then go to sleep and wake up in your grave or something. There's a purpose to your life. There's a reason why you're in this world. You are here to fulfil that purpose, and in order for you to fulfil that purpose, you have been given unique talents and abilities, which are really unique to you. You may be so good at these unique talents and abilities that you don't even recognise them as your talents and abilities, because you think, "Well, really? Is that really a talent? Is that really an ability? Isn't everyone good at that?" But it is.

This could be anything, from someone who's very good at organising, from somebody who's good at crochet, at healing, bowling and football or singing. You have this unique talent and ability, which is provided to you, so with that you can go and fulfil your life's purpose. Every single one of us, remember every single one of us has a purpose to fulfil. There is no random thing here. Nothing happens randomly in the Universal world. Everything happens for a precise reason. All of the planets have lined up for a precise reason, nature works in a precise way, there is actually law and order to everything in the Universe, absolutely everything.

Do you think that your existence on this planet is a coincidence? Do you think it was a coincidence that your parents got together and the two DNAs were fused and you were brought into this world? Do you think that was a coincidence? Absolutely NOT! The very fact of who you are right now and what experiences your parents had, which they've passed on to you: what kind of programming you received, what kind of place you are in at this very moment, the kind of people you came into contact with, everything is part of the great, grand Divine Design.

Now God's gifts to you are these dormant and sometimes latent, hidden talents and abilities. Your responsibility is to recognise them and cultivate them and nurture those talents and abilities. One of my biggest talents, I think, is that I'm able to connect with people's energy. I really am able to connect very, very quickly, and because I'm able to do that, I can remove their blocks. That's one of my biggest assets. I remove someone's energy blocks, because I can connect with their energy and then help facilitate energy shift, thereby removing their energy blocks.

However, I've got other things, for instance I'm very sociable. I love to talk. I understand great things. I'll give you another example. I'm severely dyslexic. One of the beautiful, beautiful gifts I received from dyslexia was my ability to see things from a different perspective, and to see the larger picture. Therefore when I study, I am a lot slower, yet I comprehend the concepts at a much, much deeper level. By the way, I think for me, dyslexia has been one of the biggest gifts I've received from Divine Source Energy. Because of my dyslexia, I have to see things in a different way, otherwise I couldn't learn. So I had to learn to learn in a different way. I had to study hard. It gave me the work ethic (which is something that is still with me and that is the reason for my success in all my ventures). My friends would study a chapter in half an hour. It would take me two, sometimes three hours to read the same chapter.

Dyslexia gave me the ability and talent to see things and work out things in a different way. I mean, I see things... in really large complex problems, I see very simple solutions. That's the reason why my tools and technologies are so simple because I look at something that is very complex and make a simple solution. Then I give it to my clients and to people in general when I'm working with them.

That all comes from dyslexia because I couldn't focus on one particular thing. When you focus on one particular thing too much, you can't see the bigger picture. When you can't see the bigger picture, and you can't see a bigger solution. I am unable to look at a small individual picture. I have to step back. I have to do mind mapping. I mean, mind mapping is quite famous now, quite popular. I started learning mind mapping when I was 18, 19, when it wasn't even known, in the mid-nineties. I learned speed reading and other things. I had to go through and allow my brain to develop and grow in a way so that I could learn. If I didn't have dyslexia, I would not be where I am right now. I treat being called dyslexic as a badge of honour. I am extremely proud of all that I have achieved whilst being dyslexic. If someone makes fun of my spellings , (and it still happens!) I usually respond with a laugh and remind them, that's ok, I am dyslexic. Seriously, I laugh about it, because if there's a spelling mistake, I won't recognise it. Because I assume that's the right spelling and the way I'm spelling it in my head is wrong.

I have other issues. My left and right, I can't figure out for the life of me, which is left and which is right. I really can't. And then watching yourself on camera makes it even worse, because I'm like, "Huh? Which is right, which is left?" But that doesn't matter. These are small things. It used to annoy me when I was younger, but now they don't bug me at all because I've seen the grand scheme of things. I've realised how much of a benefit being dyslexic has been for me. It's a major, major, major benefit. It's a major gift from Divine Source Energy to me, to help me to cultivate the rest of my talents, to cultivate the rest of who I am. And this is my point to you. The seventh law dictates that you have to actually recognise, what is your Divine Design? If you don't recognise it right now, you need to actually ask for guidance, ask Divine Source Energy, ask Universal Energy to show you, what is your true talent? What is your Divine Design? Show me the path, for me to go down that path. Why? Because the easiest way for you to make money is actually applying your talents and abilities to this Divine Design. That's the easiest way for you to make money. For that to happen, you have to recognise, one, that you have a Divine Design and two, recognise your unique talents and abilities. I promise you that when you're using your unique talents and abilities, doing the work is actually fun.

I'm talking all day long. I've been doing discovery calls all this week to fill up the Mastermind. Every single call has been like talking to a friend of mine, regardless of whether they've signed up or not. For this reason - I enjoy what I do. So I achieved a multi-six-figure launch this time. I'm quite happy and quite pleased with that, but it's been the easiest money I've ever made. Making money for me is very, very easy. Why? Because I love what I do. I love talking to people. I love helping them, and that's why. You need to work out, what are your unique talents and abilities? And then ask Divine Source Energy to help you to figure out how you can monetise them. Within the process, work out what is your Divine Design?

I openly say that I recognise my Divine Design... the Universe has put me on this planet to actually sort out people's energy around money. I really believe that I'm here to take all these negative ideas about money, the energy about money, and to actually change people's energy, perception and ideas about money. That's my Divine purpose. To open up peoples' hearts to abundance in all forms and allow people to live a fulfilled and abundant life. It's not living this life as a drag, as a misery, as a test. To see this life as a true gift from Divine Source Energy and to live it in a prosperous way in all forms possible. That's my Divine Design. What's yours?

The seventh law is that there is a Divine Design that is for you, that is for every single person, and every single person is different. You have your own unique talents and abilities and the easiest way for you to make money, the easiest way for you to bring money into your life is to cultivate your talents and abilities and monetise those unique talents and abilities.

Now there's a question that gets asked of me, "Well, Gull, I have many talents and abilities. How do I know which one to choose?" Again, we've gone through this. We covered this last chapter, ask your intuition. You use Law number six, which is Divine Inspiration. You may have three or four different talents. You may be good at singing. You may be good at dancing. You may be good at pottery. You may be good at maths. Then you seek Divine Inspiration, Divine Universal Energy. Using whatever name you want to give it. For me, o Divine Source Energy is Allah SWT, because I'm Muslim. You can say Brahma or Ganesha or whatever, if you're Hindu and so forth. Or

Jesus Christ or whatever name you're going to give to Divine Source Energy. It's entirely up to you.

Form that connection, and ask for inspiration. Say, "OK, which one of my talents should I monetise?" You can monetise a couple. For example, if you're good at maths and you're good at singing, then you can do your books and deal with money pretty well, because you need to have a business, obviously. For business, you have to have a head for maths, or at least hire somebody with a head for maths. You are able to oversee them and then you can sing. Or you may be great at singing and dancing, so you put those two together, right? Or you may be good at singing and dancing, but you feel that the way you can do poetry, nobody else on the planet can do it or you have a unique stance. You do poetry, and then singing and dancing are kept for you to have fun and have a laugh at.

It doesn't really matter. Ask Divine Source Energy to give you inspiration. What are your unique talents and abilities? How can you monetise it and show you the way? Then expect an answer. It is really crucial to expect an answer. Ask the question, "Divine Source Energy, where should I go? What talent should I monetise? What should I be going at? What's the easiest way for me to show my Divine self-expression? Give me guidance." And then expect an answer.

Now on the flip side, I have a lot of people saying this to me. They say, "Well, Gull, it's okay that you say that, but I don't really have any talents and abilities. I don't think I'm very good at anything." I think, "What a load of BS." There is no way. Divine Source Energy does not play favourites. The reason why your skin colour is the colour it is, or the reason why you're in this country or that country, or the reason why you're poor, rich, whatever it is, is because of the soul contract you have. We're not going to talk about soul contracts now, that's another topic for another day. But there is a reason why you're born where you are, into that family, for the particular lessons that you're here to learn.

When it comes to actually giving you talents and abilities, Divine Source Energy is very fair. Every single person has a unique talent and ability which no one else on the planet has, or has it the way that you have it. You're unique in every respect. The only thing that's holding you back is not the lack of talent; it's actually the lack of recognition. You don't recognise how powerful you are. You don't recognise how talented you are, and therefore you're holding yourself up. And you're blaming it on Divine Source Energy. That is absolutely rubbish.

Divine Source Energy has given you the best gift possible, which is this life. It has given you a soul, this gift of experiencing physical life in this physical body. That's all you're doing really. You're experiencing the physical life in this 3D world, this three-dimensional world, in this physical body, because that's what your soul came into experience, the physical experience which you're having. Now, you have been given the talents. Divine Source Energy has done two things. It's given you a Divine Design. You're here to do a particular purpose. You're supposed to do a particular thing. And in order for you to fulfil that role, you have been given unique talents and abilities. Now you've also been given willpower. So it's up to you to recognise what unique talents and abilities you have and how you can apply them to this unique Divine Design that Divine Source Energy has for you.

Most people don't do this. The reason why most people don't make money, and they get stuck again and again, is because they're not using their unique talents and abilities. They don't believe that they have this special purpose. They don't know that their unique talents and abilities are there for that particular purpose. They just think, "Okay, I'm not good at singing. I'm not good at writing. I'm not a lawyer. I'm not this. I haven't won the lottery." They keep making excuses for not living the life that they want to.

You are awesome. You are brilliant. You are fabulous just because you are who you are, you are what you are. I don't care if you're black, white, purple, green, yellow, whatever you are, you are unique and fabulous just the way you are. Your physical attributes have nothing to do with you being fabulous. Your physical skin colour, your hair colour, your eye colour, has nothing to do with how powerful you are. Nothing. You, your soul, is extremely powerful. Recognise that.

You can hear the passion in myself, in my voice and my mannerisms, how strongly I want you to understand how beautiful, how wonderful, how amazing you are. And there's only one of you, okay? I'm so sick and tired of people saying, "Well, I'm not good at anything." For God's sake, there's only one of you. God does not make mistakes. Divine Source Energy does not make mistakes. There are no coincidences. You are here for a reason. If you don't recognise that reason or you don't accept it, that's another story. You are here for a reason. You're here for a purpose. You're here to do something, which only you can do. You have a role in this grand Universal Plan.

For example, compare yourself to Richard Branson. You think, "God, what the hell do you think I am? Look at Richard Branson. He's amazing. He has his multi-billion dollar companies. He's fabulous. He travels the world. He's spiritual. He's this, he's that." And yes he is that awesome, by the way. If you're reading this, Richard Branson, I love you. You know I love you, right?

Okay. Jokes apart, he's awesome. Hands down, he's awesome. Now let's look at Richard Branson in the grand scale of things. He is a human being who is a billionaire, or one of the most famous people and one of the most amazing people on the planet. But he's only one person on this planet. We are one planet in a group of about eight planets. Eight? I can't remember now how many planets we have. I've forgotten how many planets, because I think Pluto's gone off, right? In this Milky Way. In this part of our immediate galaxy. That galaxy is part of our Universe in this third dimension.

There are multiple dimensions. There are multiple Universes. We don't actually exist in a universe. Quantum physics proves this, and science tells us there are Multiverses. There's not just a Universe. Don't believe it? Go and research something on Google on physics. We are not a Universe, we are a Multiverse.

Now imagine the Multiverse, bring it back to the Universe, bring it back to our galaxy, bring it back to our Milky Way. Bring it back to our solar system. Bring it back to our planet. And then think of one person. Yeah, one person. So now, we're on that planet and there's one person called Richard Branson. Tell me how wonderful he is now. I'm not saying he's not wonderful, by the way, I think he's awesome. I think he's brilliant. But I've just compared for you, he's this tiny speck in the grand scale of things. How much of a difference is between him and you now? Can you see the difference? The difference is in your head, the difference is in your perception. The difference is the way you're looking upon things. He is fantastic and fabulous, but he's just one tiny speck in this grand scale of Divine Design. This is a point that I want you to recognise and absolutely believe with every cell in your body, that you are the same soul that he is.

He's absolutely done a fantastic job. He's monetised his unique talents and abilities, and he's living his Divine Design. Which means if you live your Divine Design, which is cultivating your unique talents and abilities, you will get to a place which is far greater than where you are at the moment. Does that make sense? I hope it does.

Let's Recap;

This chapter is all about recognising the fact that you have a Divine Design. There is a Divine Design for every single person, every single child, mother, father, woman, everyone, everything on the planet. From the moment you you're born to the point you die, you have a purpose. There is a Divine Design for every tree, for every animal, for everything, because the Universe does not make mistakes. The Universe does not have room for error. There's a Divine Design for absolutely everything.

Not only do you have your Divine Design, you have your unique talents and abilities. And the easiest way for you to make money is to monetise those unique talents and abilities and discover how you can apply those unique talents and abilities to this Divine Design. Ask for guidance in the process. I'm not asking you to just wake up one day, and think, "Okay, this is my talent. I'm going to do this." No, ask for Divine Guidance, ask for Divine help, and you will be given the Divine guidance. You will be given the Divine help.

Trust me, when you start applying your unique talent and abilities to the Divine Design that's been made for you, you will prosper in ways that you cannot even imagine. Not only will you attract money and prosperity and financial security, you will attract love, affection, friendships and health, so abundance in all forms. That is the beauty, and that is the ultimate goal for me as a guide for you. I want you to achieve abundance in every area of your life, not just in your financial life. And when you apply the Law of Divine Design, that is when you reach out to Divine Source Energy and say, "Okay, I know you have a purpose for me. Show me what it is." If you don't have any talents ask, "Show me what talents I have for this." Or ask, "Okay, I have many talents. What talents are the most suitable for this Divine Design?" You will receive an answer. I promise you that.

That was the ninth chapter on the subject of prosperity, and we've covered all the Laws of Money. Please go back and reread all of the different laws that we have covered.

Conclusion

I hope this book has been beneficial to you, useful to you, and it's actually inspired you to take greater action and really go out and change your relationship with money. Until the next time we speak, until the next time I see you, I'm going to love you and leave you. Do come and connect with me on social media there is a list below of all my social media handles. DO come and comment there to tell me what you think of the book and even what your unique talents and abilities are, and what you think is your Divine Design. Have you found your Divine Design, and if not, how are you asking you for help, how are you seeking help? And has this chapter; has this book motivated you to go out and seek guidance on your Divine Design, on your true life purpose, as well as your talent and abilities?

Until the next time we meet, I am sending you love and blessing with an abundance of prosperity in every area of your life, especially money. Love and blessings.

THE LAWS OF MONEY ONLINE COURSE

Here's a special message from Gull Khan...

If you want to succeed with attracting more money and success into your life, then pay very close attention!

Many Spiritual workers suffer from the idea that that "If I just work harder then I'll crack it." But nothing could be further from the truth. If you're a spiritual person who wants to help more people, then this is exactly what you're looking for.

I'd like to introduce you to "The Laws of Money" – the online course that shows you how to let go of your love/hate relationship with money!

- Meet your Conscious, Subconscious and Superconscious minds...

- You'll realise that there are no malicious forces judging or punishing you...

- Stop worrying about "where the money is going to come from"...

- Make money your best friend...

- Enjoy complete calmness around your money and finances...

... and much, MUCH more!

And what makes this even better? Now you never have to deal with using the Laws of Money against you because you don't know how they work. Which also means you're not stuck with feeling like that the Laws are always working, but you're probably not in alignment with them anymore...

And best of all... you'll start seeing results with "The Laws of Money" within days.

- The sooner you learn these laws the sooner you'll see the benefits.

- This course will change how you feel about money within days.

- You will learn how to manifest more money in your life using natural laws.

And "The Laws of Money" hold the key to your success with attracting more money and success into your life.

Get access today at www.lawsofmoneyprogram.com

Printed in Great Britain
by Amazon

61910336R00119